KIN-CHAAAN!
TIME TO GET UP!
YOU'VE GOTTA GO TO YOUR GRADUATION!
YOU WOULDN'T WANNA BE LATE, NOW WOULD YOU?

I'M NOT GOING.
SHWIF...
YOU CAN'T MEAN THAT.
YOU *HAVE* TO GO TODAY.
IT'S YOUR LAST DAY OF HIGH SCHOOL EVER!

DON'T YOU WANT TO SAY GOODBYE TO ALL YOUR TEACHERS AND FRIENDS?
YOU CAN GET THEM TO SIGN YOUR GRADUATION YEARBOOK.
AND MAYBE THERE'S A GIRL THERE WHO WANTS THE SECOND BUTTON OF YOUR BLAZER.
THERE IS, ISN'T THERE?

NO.
NO?
MAYBE THERE IS, THOUGH.
ANYWAY, I'VE GOTTA GET TO WORK.
SORRY I CAN'T MAKE YOUR GRADUATION, SWEETIE.
PAT PAT
NOW EAT SOME BREAKFAST AND GET YOUR BUTT TO SCHOOL.
LIGHT A STICK OF INCENSE FOR GRANDMA ON YOUR WAY OUT, TOO.
BYE!
CLICK

March 14 (Friday)
2014
7:21

HEY, GRAND-MA.

I'M HEADING OUT.

BRR!
HWOOOO
ヒュオォ…
NAO-KUN HASN'T BEEN HIMSELF SINCE POCHI DIED.
HIS TEACHER CALLED AND SOUNDED REALLY WORRIED, TOO.
HEY, NAO. WANT YOUR OLD MAN TO TAKE YOU TO SCHOOL?
GASP はっ
GASP はっ
スタ SHUF
SHUF スタ
…
…
Shh!
Oh! It's that blond guy.
スタ SHUF

IT'S IMAMURA-SAN'S SON.
HE'S GOT SOME NERVE, DOESN'T HE? GOING TO SCHOOL LIKE THAT.
NAO'S ALWAYS BEEN AFRAID OF HIM, TOO.
IT MAKES ME UNCOMFORTABLE. WHERE ARE THE TEACHERS?
THAT GUY'S NOSE IS RUNNING.
PANT
PANT
PANT
PANT
PANT
SHH!
ガッ TMP
EEK!
THUUUNK バタン
PLONK むくっ...
OWWW...

...

FWAP

CRAP!

ZOOM!

GAH!

IMAMURA!

FLINCH

WHAT ARE YOU DOING, AKI?

AGGGH, THAT WAS CLOSE!

I THOUGHT HE WAS GONNA KILL ME!

SHAKE

SHAKE

WE'VE NEVER EVEN TALKED BEFORE, BUT I JUST SAID HIS NAME WITHOUT THINKING!

HA HA HA HA HA
DON'T WORRY ABOUT IT.
IMAMURA'S NOT AS SCARY AS HE LOOKS.
WELL, THAT'S TRUE, BUT I JUST CAN'T FIGURE OUT WHAT HIS PROBLEM IS.
Y'know?
I mean, it's not like he's in a gang or something, so why's he go around looking like that?

HE HASN'T MADE A SINGLE FRIEND OVER THE LAST THREE YEARS, RIGHT?
HE LIVED IN TOKYO UNTIL MIDDLE SCHOOL, IF I REMEMBER. I DON'T THINK HE KNEW ANYONE AROUND TOWN.
AND HE NEVER SO MUCH AS TALKED TO A GIRL, DID HE? THEY ALL JUST AVOIDED HIM.
IT'S LIKE, WHY WAS HE EVEN COMING TO SCHOOL?

SAITAMA PREFECTURE KABOSU MINAMI HIGH SCHOOL GRADUATE DIPLOMA CONFERRAL CEREMONY
HEY...
BWA HA HA HA
...
whisper whisper whisper
ヒソヒソヒソ...
WHOA...
...DON'T YOU THINK?
ボリボリボリ...
SCRITCH SCRITCH SCRITCH
IMA-MURA!
HALT ッ...

...
KITAJIMA-SENSEI.
YOU REALLY CAME TO YOUR GRADUATION WITH YOUR HAIR LOOKING LIKE THAT? IT'S A MESS.
YOU'RE BEING DISRUPTIVE.
...
WHAT'S THE PROBLEM?
A LOT OF PARENTS ARE GOING TO SHOW UP TODAY.
YOU'RE GONNA STICK OUT LIKE A SORE THUMB.
FWIP
...

PWINK
HOW ABOUT NOW?
HEY!
MUCH BETTER THAN BEFORE. I LIKE IT!
CLAP CLAP

BOY, IMAMURA, YOU SURE HAVE GOTTEN BIG SINCE YOU FIRST STARTED COMING HERE.
IF ONLY YOU'D JOINED A SPORTS CLUB OR SOMETHING. WHAT A WASTE!

WASN'T THERE AT LEAST ONE THAT YOU WANTED TO TRY?

NOPE.
I...
...WAS NEVER PARTICULARLY INTERESTED IN ANY OF THAT.
PAT PAT

ALL RIGHT, ALL RIGHT.

WELL, YOU'VE WORKED HARD THESE LAST THREE YEARS.
CONGRATULATIONS, GRADUATE.

Diploma
SACHIKO SAKURAI
BORN FEBRUARY 9, 1996
The person named above has graduated from our school's foreign languages department.
MARCH 14, 2014
PRINCIPAL OF SAITAMA PREFECTURE KABOSU MINAMI H
GRADUATE #29056

GRADUATE DIPLOMA CONFERRAL CEREMONY
SAITAMA PREFECTURE KABOSU MINAMI HIGH SCHOOL
I CAN'T BELIEVE THIS IS OUR GRADUATION.
HAVE THEY POSTED WHO GOT IN YET?
I'M SLEEPY.
GOD, THIS SURE DOESN'T FEEL LIKE THE END.

AAWWW, I WISH I TOLD NOJIMA-KUN I LIKED HIM... THIS SUCKS ...
GET HIM TO GIVE YOU HIS SECOND BUTTON. THERE'S STILL TIME!
THIRD YEAR, CLASS C.
I GAVE UP ON THE SOCCER CLUB, SO I DON'T EVEN HAVE ANY KOHAI.
THAT'S JUST HOW IT IS, MAN. OUR SENPAI SUCKED ASS.
THIRD YEAR, CLASS D.
MASAHIRO ARITA.
HERE.
AGGGH!
I NEVER EVEN GOT A GIRLFRIEND.
KINICHIRO IMAMURA.

CLATTER
... HERE.

HEY, THE FIRST CHARACTER IN "KINICHIRO" MEANS GOLD, AND HE HAS GOLD HAIR ...
I CAN'T EVEN THINK OF A PUNCHLINE FOR THAT.
GIGGLE
It's just too obvious.
WHERE'S IMAMURA GOING FROM HERE?
HE DIDN'T APPLY TO COLLEGE, RIGHT?

ACCORDING TO OUR TEACHER ...
...HE DOESN'T EVEN HAVE A JOB LINED UP.
FOR REAL?
WHAT'S HE EVEN WANT TO DO?
GRADUATING FROM *THIS* SCHOOL WITHOUT ANY PLANS ABOUT WHAT TO DO NEXT? LIKE, NO ONE DOES THAT!
DAMN.

I MEAN, NOT THAT I CARE. IT'S NOT LIKE I'M FRIENDS WITH HIM.
HARSH! HAHA

くるっ
TURN
MUTTER
MUTTER
MUTTER
MUTTER
...HEY.
C'MON, GET DOWN.
はっ
GASP
バッ
RUSH
OH, YEAH ...

122ND GRADUATE DIPLOMA CONFERRAL CEREMONY
SAITAMA PREFECTURE KABOSU MINAMI HIGH SCHOOL
AND NOW, THE SCHOOL SONG.
DOOO
DOOO
DOO
DOOOOO
THREE YEARS AGO, AT MY ENTRANCE CEREMONY ...
... THAT GIRL SANG THE SCHOOL SONG ON STAGE.
SHE WAS SO DAMN LOUD.

WHAT DID SHE LOOK LIKE, AGAIN?
LET'S TAKE A PICTURE TOGETHER!
LET ME IN ON THIS!
YAY!
I THINK...
THE OUENDAN'S CLUB ROOM WAS AROUND HERE.
OUR SCHOOL HAD AN OUENDAN UNTIL MY FIRST YEAR HERE.
I ONLY EVER GOT TO SEE THEM AT MY ENTRANCE CEREMONY.

I HEAR NOT A SINGLE PERSON IN MY YEAR JOINED THE CLUB,

AND THAT'S WHY IT'S GONE NOW.

THERE'S AN OLD BUILDING OF THE SCHOOL'S WHERE THEIR FORMER CLUB ROOM STILL REMAINS AND—WELL, IT REMAINS.

I'D HAVE TO KNOW SOMEONE TO KNOW ANYTHING MORE THAN THAT.

DO NOT ENTER
ENTER
ギィ
CREAK
HEY!
IT'S UN-LOCKED.

CLAT

CLAT

PHOTOGRAPHY CLUB
HEY, THERE ARE OTHER CLUBS IN HERE, TOO.
SCHOOL WORKING GROUPS
LET'S SEE ...

OUENDAN
THERE IT IS!

OUENDAN
ガチャ
CHACK
ガチャ
KACHACK
DAMN ...
LOCKED, HUH ...

OUENDAN

...

HUP!
...
I'D LIKE...
...TO SEE IT ONE LAST TIME.
THUNK
KATHUNK
HRGH!
HRGH!
OKAY.
SHUMP
HIRO-KUN,
WHAT ARE YOU DOING?
LITERATURE CLUB

WAIT ...
?!
YOU'RE ...
FROM THIS MOR-NING ...
I- I DIDN'T SEE ANY-THING!
SHUF
I'M JUST TRYING TO MEET UP WITH MY BOY-FRIEND ...
JUST, PRETEND I'M NOT HERE ... Y'KNOW ...
I PROMISE I WON'T TELL ANYONE ABOUT THIS ...
SHUF SHUF
HEY.
I THINK YOU'VE GOT THE WRONG IDEA.
Uhh, you see...

PERVEEERT!
JUMP
HEY, WAIT!
THMP
QUIT TRYING TO RUN!
AGH!
NOOOOOOOOO
TURN
WAIT UP! GOD!

HEEEEY!

C'MON, ANSWER ME!

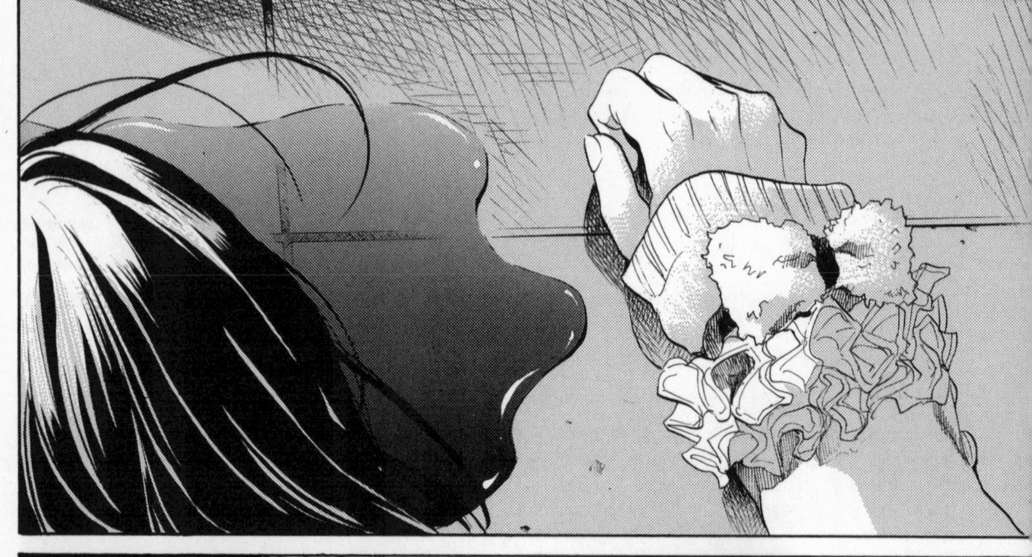
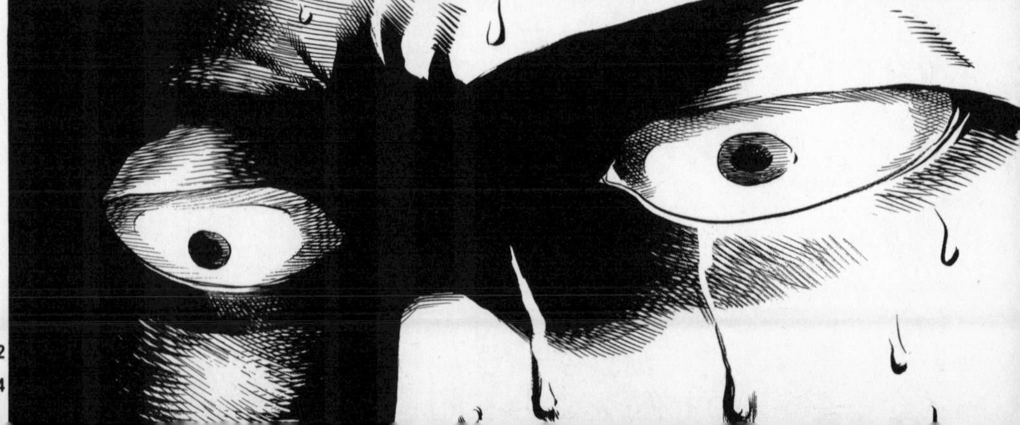

HEY!!
SLIP
?!
TUNK
TUNK
TMP
TMP

THWUNK
AGGGGGH...

DAMN IT.
JUST...
LOOK AT ME.
I KNEW IT.
NOTHING GOOD EVER COMES OF ME TRYING TO SOCIALIZE.
AGGGH...
EVERY-ONE...
WE WOULDN'T HAVE LOST IF IT WEREN'T FOR YOU.
THIS IS WHAT ALWAYS HAPPENS.
NOTHING GOOD EVER COMES OF HAVING YOU AROUND, IMAMURA.
DON'T WORRY, KIN-CHAN. IT'S NOT YOUR FAULT.
WE TOLD YOU NOT TO COME TO SCHOOL.
WHY DIDN'T YOU LISTEN?
IF IT WEREN'T FOR YOU.

EVERYONE...
I'M SO SORRY.
...CHAN.
KIN-CHAN, TIME TO GET UP!
YOU'LL BE LATE FOR SCHOOL.
OH.
ぱ
SNAP

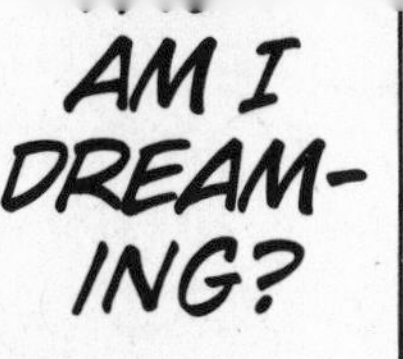
AM I DREAMING?

NOW, HURRY UP AND EAT YOUR BREAKFAST.
IT'S LEFTOVER CURRY FROM LAST NIGHT.
WE DIDN'T HAVE CURRY LAST NIGHT.

OH!
I'LL GET YOU SOME MISO SOUP, MOM.
WANT ANY PICKLED VEGETABLES?
NOD NOD

GRANDMA?
HUH ?!
?

WAIT, YOU MUST JUST LOOK LIKE HER, RIGHT?
DAMN, THOUGH! YOU SCARED ME!

KIN-CHAN, HAVE YOU BEEN GETTING ENOUGH SLEEP?

MOM...
HAVE YOU GAINED WEIGHT?
And cut your hair?

THAT'S RUDE!
I'VE LOST WEIGHT RECENTLY, FOR YOUR INFORMATION!
YOU DEFINITELY GAINED WEIGHT.
FLAIL

WHATEVER! JUST GET YOUR BUTT TO SCHOOL.
SCRITCH SCRITCH
HUH?
WHY SHOULD I GO TO SCHOOL?

YOU WOULDN'T WANNA BE LATE ON YOUR FIRST DAY, NOW WOULD YOU?!

UHH ...
WHAT ?
WHEN ... DID I GET MY HAIR CUT?

...
...

PERHAPS I OUGHT TO ACCOMPANY KIN-CHAN TO HIS ENTRANCE CEREMONY.
HE ... COULD BE LONELY ON HIS OWN, DON'T YOU THINK?

UGGGH, COME ON, MOM! KIN-CHAN'S IN HIS FIRST YEAR OF HIGH SCHOOL NOW.
OH!
IS HE REALLY, NOW?
MY PHONE ...
GOTTA CHECK MY PHONE.
IS THIS DREAM ...

pril 6 (Wednesday)
2011

...TAKING PLACE THREE YEARS AGO?

HUH. I GUESS THEY HADN'T BUILT THAT CONVE-NIENCE STORE YET.

YOU SHOULD GO WALK POCHI WITH NAO, DEAR.
YOU'VE GOTTA LOSE SOME WEIGHT.
RIGHT?
YEAH, DAD. YOU'RE FAT.
GUH ...

IT'S NOT REALLY A DREAM ...
...IT'S MORE LIKE I'M RELIVING MY MEMO-RIES.

SAITAMA PREFECTURE KABOSU MINAMI HIGH SCHOOL ENTRANCE CEREMONY
WELL ...
I NEVER THOUGHT I'D HAVE TO COME BACK HERE AGAIN. IT IS JUST A DREAM, THOUGH ...
WHO'S THAT GUY?
I DON'T KNOW.
I DON'T REMEMBER SEEING HIM IN MIDDLE SCHOOL, DO YOU?
HE'S SCARY.
WHISPER WHISPER
JUST LIKE ... BACK THEN.
IF I REMEMBER RIGHT, THAT SHOULD MEAN ...
... I WALK UP TO THE FRONT GATE, AND ...
Let's see...

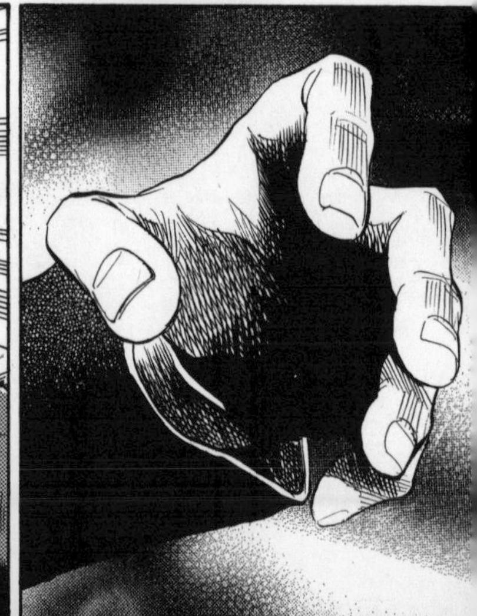

TELL ME YOUR NAME, SON.
WHAT IS IT?
IMA-MURA.
NOW, IT'S TRUE THAT WE TRY TO FOSTER INDEPENDENCE IN OUR STUDENTS HERE BY NOT BEING TOO STRICT,
BUT TODAY'S THE ENTRANCE CEREMONY, AND I IMAGINE A PARENT OR TWO MIGHT HAVE SOMETHING TO SAY...
...ABOUT THAT BLOND HAIR OF YOURS.
OHHH YEAH. I REMEMBER THIS.

THREE YEARS AGO, I THOUGHT I WAS GETTING FUSSED AT AND FREAKED OUT.
YEAH...
SO ?!
WHO GIVES A CRAP?
HE GOT MADDER THAN HE NEEDED TO.
THREE YEARS AGO

UHH...

OH, BUT I'M NOT BREAKING ANY RULES, AM I?
It's just fashion. I'm not trying to make a statement.
I'M NOT A DELINQUENT, AND IT'S NOT LIKE I HAVE A PROBLEM WITH SOCIETY OR ANYTHING. I'VE NEVER EVEN GOTTEN VIOLENT WITH ANYONE, SO YOU DON'T NEED TO WORRY.

ALL RIGHT, ALL RIGHT.
I GET IT.
I'M THE GUIDANCE COUNSELOR HERE, KITAJIMA.
NICE TO MEET YOU!

FLINCH
ビク
What's with that bag, huh?
Mor-ning!
Sor-ry!
HE REALLY ISN'T THE TYPE WHO LIKES TO SCOLD PEOPLE, IS HE?
I learned that later on.

EVERYONE AT THIS SCHOOL IS SO NORMAL AND DILIGENT.
I GUESS THAT'S WHY THEY AVOIDED ME FROM DAY ONE.

I WENT THROUGH THREE YEARS OF THAT.

AND THAT'S ALL.

ISN'T SHE CUTE?

WHISPER

WHO DO YOU LIKE IN OUR CLASS?

...

THERE'S SUZUKI, THE GUY WHO BROKE HIS KNEE PLAYING BASEBALL FIRST THING AND COULD NEVER GET A GIRLFRIEND.
AND THERE'S SATO. SHE WAS THE QUIETEST AND MOST HARD-WORKING STUDENT IN OUR YEAR, BUT SHE FAILED HER UNIVERSITY ENTRANCE EXAMS WHEN THE COLLEGE STUDENT WHO WAS TUTORING HER DUMPED HER.

LET'S SEE... I FORGOT THAT ONE'S NAME, BUT THINGS DIDN'T GO WELL FOR HER ONCE SHE GAINED FIFTEEN KILOS.

HIS HOUSE CATCHES ON FIRE.
OH, AND THAT ONE? HMM...

EVERYONE'S SO EXCITED AND HOPEFUL ABOUT STARTING HIGH SCHOOL ...
... BUT I'VE GOT NEWS FOR YOU IDIOTS: IT AIN'T GONNA WORK OUT.

SQUEEEEEZE
IF THIS IS A DREAM, THEN LET ME WAKE UP ALREADY!

IT'S NOT LIKE I HAVE ANY GOOD MEMORIES OF THIS PLACE, EITHER!
NEXT, THE SCHOOL SONG.

AND NOW,
WE PRESENT A WELCOMING CHEER FROM THE OUENDAN FOR OUR NEW STUDENTS.
ばっ
FWIP
I CAN...
...MEET HER.
ス
SHF
THAT'S RIGHT.

THE HELL ?
MUTTER
HUH ?
MUTTER
A GIRL ?
BADUMP

SAITAMA PREFECTURE KABOSU MINAMI HIGH SCHOOL
OUENDAN
CLENCH
PREFECTURE KABOSU MINAMI HIGH SCHOOL
FWOO

LET THE FIGHT SONG BEGIN!
DOOOO!
DOO!
DOOOO!
DOOO
DOOOO
DOOOO
DOOOOO!
DOOOO
DOOO
DOOO
DOOO
THE CHERRRRRY TREES BEGIIIN TO BLOOOM
AND THEIR SCEEENT IS ON THE WIIIND

WH-PISH!
WH-PISH!
WHEN THE WIIINGS OF FREEEEEDOM
MAAAAY TAKE
FLIIIGHT
JEEZ, WHAT A VOICE...
I DIDN'T KNOW THIS SCHOOL HAD AN OUENDAN.
WHY IS THE CAPTAIN A GIRL?
GOD...
I FEEL EMBARRASSED JUST WATCHING.
FOR REAL.
WATCHING SOMEONE GO WAY OVER THE TOP ALL ON THEIR OWN LIKE THAT...
...IS PAINFUL.
NO ONE HAS AN OUENDAN THESE DAYS.
OHHH MAY TRUTH AND LOVE UNITE AS ONE
THREE YEARS AGO...
I THOUGHT THE SAME THING.
NO ONE TAKES THE SCHOOL SONG SERIOUSLY,
SO IT SEEMED RIDICULOUS TO GO UP ON STAGE AND SING IT AT THE TOP OF YOUR LUNGS.

NO ONE FELT LIKE THEY NEEDED HER TO CHEER FOR THEM...

...AND YET SHE KEPT AT IT ALL BY HERSELF. I NEVER DID FIND OUT WHY.

SINCE SHE WAS...

...THE OUENDAN'S LAST CAPTAIN.

COME CHECK OUT THE SOCCER CLUB!
KANAN HIGH SOCCER CLUB
LITERATU CLUB
ARTS CRAFT CLUB
THINK THE ARTS AND CRAFTS CLUB IS BORING?
HEY, YOU. HOW ABOUT IT?
EVERY-ONE IN OUR CLUB IS REAL CLOSE.
GET OVER

IF I'VE GONE BACK TO THAT TIME THREE YEARS AGO...
IF SHE'S GOING TO TALK TO ME AGAIN...
THERE'S SOMETHING...
...I'VE ALWAYS WANTED TO ASK HER.

HEY, MAN. WITH HAIR LIKE THAT, YOU'D BE PERFECT FOR THE OUENDAN.

WHY DON'T YOU TRY IT?

JUST LIKE THREE YEARS AGO!
HEY, MAN. WITH HAIR LIKE THAT, YOU'D BE PERFECT FOR THE OUENDAN.
WHY DON'T YOU TRY IT?
UH ...
BACK THEN...
...I JUST PANICKED AND RAN AWAY, THOUGH.

SHF

I WONDER ...

...

IS ...

...IT FUN TO BE IN THE OUENDAN?

?!
GRAB
OF COURSE IT'S FUN.
YOU WANT TO JOIN, DON'T YOU?
YOU'RE A MAN OF YOUR WORD, RIGHT?
UH ...
NO... I MEAN, I DON'T KNOW ...
THAT'S ONE NEW MEMBER IN THE BAG!!
GLOMP
HEY!
ARE YOU SURE ABOUT THIS?!
IF YOU'RE HAVING SECOND THOUGHTS, NOW'S THE TIME TO SAY IT!
MUTTER
FOR REAL?
Whoa...
MUTTER
?
?!
HE CAN'T BE SERIOUS ...
SOME-BODY STOP HIM.

OHHH GODDD! CALM DOWN, KINICHIRO! CALM DOWN!
YOU'RE DREAM-ING!
SQUEEZE
THAT SAID, I SURE AM TAKING MY DAMN TIME ABOUT WAKING UP.

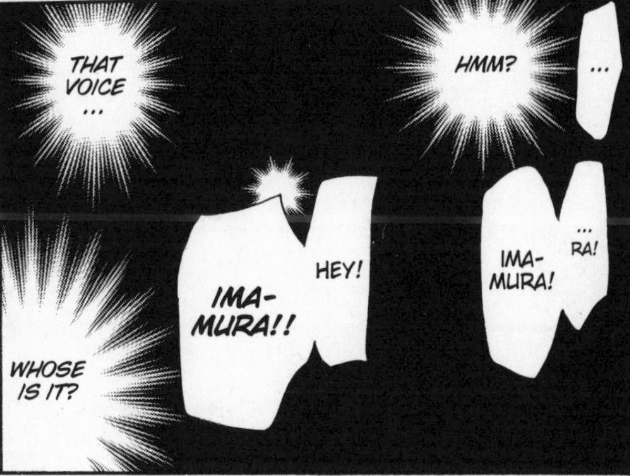
...
HMM?
THAT VOICE ...
... RA!
IMA-MURA!
HEY!
IMA-MURA!!
WHOSE IS IT?

I SAID HEY! IMA-MURA!
GRAB

GOD ...

GOOD JOB PUSHING ME DOWN THE STAIRS.

WHAT ARE YOU GONNA DO ABOUT THIS?
THANKS TO YOU ...
...WE'VE GONE BACK IN TIME THREE YEARS!
BECAUSE OF ME...
...WE'VE GONE BACK IN TIME?!
2011
NO NO NO NO NO ...
THIS ...
...MUST BE PART OF THE DREAM, RIGHT?
I'D LIKE TO WAKE UP, TOO, Y'KNOW!
SLAP
SLAP
SLAP
STUPID, STUPID, STUPID, STUPID!
SLAP

HEY.

IF YOU'VE GOT A PROBLEM WITH MY NEW MEMBER, YOU CAN TALK TO ME ABOUT IT.

EXCUSE ME? JUST WHO ARE YOU?

ME?

I SUPPOSE I HAVEN'T INTRODUCED MYSELF, HUH?

I'M THE CAPTAIN OF KABOSU MINAMI'S OUENDAN,

YOSHIKO USAMI.

SO, NEW GUY, WHAT'S YOUR NAME, AND WHAT CLASS ARE YOU IN?

NO FRIENDS, NO CLUBS, NO NOTHING.
THAT WAS HIGH SCHOOL FOR ME, BUT...
I'M KINICHIRO IMAMURA.
I'M IN CLASS 1-C...
NOW I'M SUPPOSED TO DO IT ALL OVER AGAIN?!

Again!!
アゲイン!!

2.
AKI'S SITUATION

SAITAMA PREFECTURE KABOSU MINAMI HIGH SCHOOL GRADUATE DIPLOMA CONFERRAL CEREMONY
AWW!
YOU'RE GOING OVERBOARD WITH THE CRYING, AKI.
BUT!
MARCH 14, 2014
I JUST CAN'T BELIEVE THAT I'M GRADUATING TODAY!
I WANNA STAY WITH YOU GUYS FOREVER!
OH, AKI-SENPAI!
COME VISIT US AT THE TENNIS CLUB ONCE IN A WHILE, OKAY?
I ALWAYS LOVED YOU, AKI-SENPAI!
SEN-PAI!
OHHH!
YUNA! RUMI-RUMI! ERENA!
I LOVE YOU ALL! THE TENNIS CLUB IS YOURS NOW!
BZZ BZZ BZZ BZZ
OH ...
...
CLACK

MY HIGH SCHOOL CAREER ENDS TODAY.
IT SEEMED TO TAKE FOREVER, BUT NOW IT FEELS LIKE IT PASSED IN THE BLINK OF AN EYE.
きゅん…
THROB…
HIRO-KUN…
11:04
1/1000
Inbox
11:04
03/14/14
Hiro
Let's meet up
Wait for me in the west building
-END-
MENU
SELECT

WHAT A PLACE TO MEET UP. THERE'S NO ONE ELSE HERE…
I GUESS THAT MEANS I CAN GET MY HOPES UP. ♥

CLATTER
CLATTER
CLATTER
HUH? HE'S ALREADY HERE?

PEEK

?
CLATTER
LITERATURE CLUB
CLUTTER
CLATTER

HIRO-KUN!
WHAT ARE YOU DOING?

YOU'RE ...
FROM THIS MOR-NING ...
?!
IMA-MURA ?!
HE'S SCARY-LOOKING, BLEACHES HIS HAIR BLOND, AND IS A TOTAL OUTCAST.
WHAT'S HE EVEN DOING, TRYING TO BREAK INTO AN EMPTY CLUB ROOM?
THIS SCHOOL IS TRASH !
I'LL BURN IT DOWN !
I'LL STEAL SHIT !
I'LL RAPE HER !
EEK!
...
PERVEEEEERT!
TWIRL
DASH
HEY, WAIT!

HUH ?!
OUCH ...
THIS HURTS SO BAD I COULD DIE.
WHAT THE HELL? NOT COOL.
THIS SUCKS...

I DON'T WANNA DIE!

ガバぁっ

JOLT

...HUH?

I WAS DREAMING?

DRIP DRIP

ボロボロ…

チュン…

CHIRP

チュン…

CHIRP

I FEEL LIKE I HAD SOME KIND OF NIGHTMARE, BUT WHAT WAS IT?
AKI!
BREAK-FAST IS READY! TIME TO GET UP!
OKAY!

GUH...
I THINK I'LL TAKE A SHOWER FIRST.

I CAN'T...
SLIDE
ガラッ
...REALLY REMEMBER.

SHMP
バタム…

ぎゃあああ
GAAAAH!
?!

WHAT'S WRONG?
AKI?!
BAM
BAM
BAM
...

MY BOOBS GOT SMALLER ?!

WHY ?!

YOU MUST HAVE LOST SOME WEIGHT.
ANYWAY, I'M HEADED DOWN TO THE SALON.
They're opening early for me.
DON'T FORGET TO EAT BREAK-FAST BEFORE YOU GO.
PIT PAT PIT PAT
WELL, I'LL SEE YOU AT THE EN-TRANCE CERE-MONY!
SLIDE
CLICK
?!
DID YOU SAY SOME-THING, MOM?

OH ...
SSSSSH
Huh... I don't remember cutting my hair this short...
LET'S SEE ...
I GUESS I... HAVE TO GO TO SCHOOL ?

She can be such a dork.
GOD...
WHY'D MOM PUT UP A CALENDAR FROM THREE YEARS AGO?
HUH?
WHERE'S THAT SCRUNCHIE I BOUGHT THE OTHER DAY? I REALLY LIKED IT.
ACK!
LOOK AT THE TIME!
CLAT CLAT CLAT CLAT
I'LL BE LATE TO MEET UP WITH HIRO-KUN!
THERE HE IS!
HIRO-KUUUN!
WAVE
WAVE
THAT GIRL WHO'S WITH HIRO-KUN...
HUH?

SHE'S HIS EX!
THEY WENT OUT IN MIDDLE SCHOOL AND WERE SUPPOSED TO HAVE BROKEN UP DURING OUR FIRST YEAR!
SO **WHAT** ARE THEY DOING TOGETHER **NOW?!**
じぇらっ…
JEALOUSY
WHO'S THAT?
BEATS ME.
LET'S GET OUT OF HERE.
OKAY.
EXCUSE ME?
WHAT THE HELL?
WE WERE SUPPOSED TO GO TO THE SAME COLLEGE IN TOKYO AND BE TOGETHER FOREVER!
がばっ
COLLAPSE
ASSHOLE!
HMM?
WAIT...
I GRADUATED, DIDN'T I?
HUH?

I REMEMBER NOW.
I WAS AT MY HIGH SCHOOL GRADUATION.
SO...
2cm
20/30 VISION (CONTACTS)
20/15 VISION (UNASSISTED)
B-CUP
A-CUP
THREE YEARS AGO
WHY HAS EVERYTHING, INCLUDING MY BODY, GONE BACK TO HOW IT WAS THREE YEARS AGO?
MORNING,
AKI.
SAITAMA PREFECTURE KABOSU MINAMI HIGH SCHOOL ENTRANCE CEREMONY
WE GET TO BE IN THE SAME CLASS AGAIN, JUST LIKE MIDDLE SCHOOL! PRETTY COOL, RIGHT?
WHAT CLUB ARE YOU GONNA JOIN, AKI?
SINCE WE GOT INTO A GOOD SCHOOL AND ALL, I'D LIKE TO TRY SOMETHING NEW.

YUKIKO HANAI.

HERE.

AYANO HIRATA.

HERE.

AKIRA FUJIEDA.

HERE!

OH WELL.

NOW I CAN DO HIGH SCHOOL ALL OVER AGAIN!

THESE FIRST-YEAR CLASSES WILL BE A PIECE OF CAKE,
SO I CAN JUST HAVE FUN!

MAYBE I'LL EVEN BECOME FAMOUS FOR MY ABILITY TO TELL THE FUTURE OR SOMETHING.
Wow! She got another one right!
How's she know this stuff?
CHEER
CHEER
CHEER

AND HIRO-KUN SHOULD BE BREAKING UP WITH THAT EX OF HIS BEFORE TOO LONG.
HE IS THE ONE WHO LIKED ME FIRST, AFTER ALL.
GAAAH
RAAAGE
AGH, I WANNA GO ON A BUNCH OF DATES ALREADY!

DIIING
DOOONG
DAAANG
DOOONG
CLATTER
I THINK I'LL GO PAY HIRO-KUN A VISIT!

I HAD SO MANY GREAT FRIENDS MY FIRST YEAR OF HIGH SCHOOL. THEY HAD ME LAUGHING MY ASS OFF EVERY SINGLE DAY.

HIRO-KUN!

NOW...

I GET TO EXPERIENCE IT ALL AGAIN.

FLINCH

びくっ

WHAT?

HEY! LET'S WALK HOME TOGETHER!

WE CAN STOP SOMEWHERE FOR TEA, TOO!

...WHAT? YOU'RE BEING REALLY WEIRD.

DON'T JUST CALL ME HIRO-KUN OUT OF NOWHERE.

WHO EVEN ARE YOU, ANYWAY?

I'M AKIRA FUJIEDA!

WE'RE GONNA GET ALONG REALLY WELL.

DUDE, I HATE GIRLS LIKE YOU.

NEVER TALK TO ME AGAIN.

WHAT'S WITH HER?
DAMN...
WHOA!

WHY...

...IS THIS HAPPENING TO ME?

HALT
ピタ
THAT'S ONE NEW MEMBER IN THE BAG!
THE OUENDAN GOT SOME-BODY.
DAMN, FOR REAL ?!
WASN'T THAT ...
THAT BLOND GUY ...
IMA-MURA!
GOD, GOOD JOB PUSHING ME DOWN THE STAIRS!
?!

AGGGGGH!
YOU'RE ALIVE!
WHAT ARE YOU GONNA DO ABOUT THIS?!
FLINCH
THANKS TO YOU, WE'VE GONE BACK IN TIME THREE YEARS!
GASP
WAIT ...
IMA-MURA, YOU'RE ...
FROM THE FUTURE, TOO?
BADUMP
Now that I take a good look at it, his face isn't too bad, either.

HEH...
NO NO NO NO NO ...
THIS MUST BE PART OF THE DREAM, RIGHT?
pft

GRRR
I'D LIKE TO WAKE UP, TOO, Y'KNOW! STUPID, STUPID, STUPID, STUPID!
SLAPSLAP SLAPSLAP
HEY.
IF YOU'VE GOT A PROBLEM WITH MY NEW MEMBER, YOU CAN TALK TO ME ABOUT IT.

HOW CAN YOU BE HAVING SO MUCH FUN DOING HIGH SCHOOL OVER AGAIN, IMAMURA?!

IT'S NOT LIKE YOU EVEN HAD ANY FRIENDS! YOU'RE JUST BEING A LITTLE SHIT!

UGH!

IT'S NOT FAIR!

IMA-MURA?

IS SHE A FRIEND OF YOURS?

HALT

WE FELL DOWN THE STAIRS? THAT WASN'T A DREAM?
WELL, DUH!
I THOUGHT I WAS GONNA DIE!
WHAT ARE YOU GONNA DO ABOUT THIS?
THANKS TO YOU, WE'VE GONE BACK IN TIME THREE YEARS!
NO NO NO NO NO ...
THIS MUST BE PART OF THE DREAM, RIGHT?
I'D LIKE TO WAKE UP, TOO, Y'KNOW! STUPID, STUPID, STUPID, STUPID!

WHAT ARE THEY GOING ON ABOUT?
THOSE NEW STUDENTS AREN'T MAKING ANY SENSE.
WHO'S THE BLOND GUY? HE'S SCARY-LOOKING...
IS HE IN A GANG?
THAT CUTE GIRL WON'T STOP CRYING AND YELLING. DID SOMETHING HAPPEN?
UH.
I'VE BEEN WATCHING FOR A WHILE NOW...

...AND I THINK IT'S BECAUSE THE OUENDAN GOT TOO PUSHY ABOUT RECRUITING NEW MEMBERS AGAIN.
HALT
ぴたっ
WHOA!
SUCKS FOR THEM.
HUH?

3. ULTRA-STRENGTH RECRUITING!

HEY.
WHAT WAS THAT?

EEEK!
ポイ
TOSS
STOMP ズン
STOMP ズン
STOMP ズン
SHE'S
UH-
ピシッ
SNAP!
IF YOU'VE GOT SOMETHING TO SAY, THEN SAY IT TO MY FACE.

...
I'VE BEEN HOLDING MY TONGUE ABOUT THIS FOR A LONG TIME,
BUT, FRANKLY, THE OUENDAN IS ANNOYING AS HELL.
I KNOW ALL THE OTHER CLUBS AGREE WITH ME!
ESPECIALLY SINCE YOU BECAME CAPTAIN, USAMI!
WHAT?
NO ONE EVER ASKED YOU TO CHEER FOR US.
NONE OF THE SCHOOLS WE PLAY AGAINST EVER HAVE OUENDAN, ANYWAY.
IT'S JUST EMBARRASSING.
DO YOU HAVE ANY IDEA WHAT THEY SAY ABOUT US AT OTHER HIGH SCHOOLS?
WHOA...
THEY'RE GOING A LITTLE FAR...

DON'T MAKE ME LAUGH.
?!
LIKE IT OR NOT, I'M GONNA CHASE YOU DOWN TO THE ENDS OF THE EARTH.
AND I'M NOT GONNA STOP UNTIL YOU PUNKS START WINNING!
YOU THINK YOU CAN BLAME ME FOR YOUR LOSSES? NOW THAT'S FUNNY.

MARK MY WORDS!
YOU NO-GOOD, TUITION-MONEY-WASTING BUNCH OF PATHETIC EXCUSES FOR ATHLETES!
POINT
...
LET'S GO, NEWBIES.
FWOO
HEY! WHY DO I HAVE TO GO?
WHISPER WHISPER
I DON'T WANNA GO ON MY OWN!
WHISPER WHISPER
WE'LL BE IN THE CLUB ROOM.
OSU!!
BAP BAP
FLINCH
HUH?
RIGHT.
HEY!
YOU SHOULDN'T GET INVOLVED WITH THE OUENDAN IF YOU KNOW WHAT'S GOOD FOR YOU!

HERE'S WHERE THE OUENDAN'S CLUB ROOM IS.
THEY USE THIS OLD BUILDING ON THE EDGE OF CAMPUS FOR CLUBS NOW.
MOST PEOPLE JUST CALL IT THE WEST BUILDING.
WHAT'S WRONG?
...
THIS IS WHERE...
NOTH-ING...

...WE FELL DOWN THE STAIRS AND BACK THROUGH TIME.

WHAT ...

...IF WE CAN NEVER GO BACK TO OUR OWN TIME?

SOB うっ...

DON'T KNOW. DON'T CARE.

DRIP ポロ DRIP ポロ...

WANNA TRY FALLING DOWN THERE AGAIN?

NO!

I NEVER WISHED I COULD DO HIGH SCHOOL OVER AGAIN...

GET YOUR ASSES UP THOSE STAIRS ALREADY!

OUENDAN

RADIO CLUB

BUT...

...I REALLY DIDN'T JOIN ANY CLUBS, DID I?

A TAIKO DRUM ...

WE DON'T HAVE MANY MEMBERS YET, BUT DON'T WORRY.

NOW, ENTER!

OKAY ...

DON'T FORGET TO SAY, "OSU! EXCUSE ME," AS YOU COME IN.

*SEE TRANSLATION NOTES ABOUT "OSU!" IN THE BACK OF THE BOOK.

SHOCK
I CAN'T HEAR YOU!

O-OSU! EX-CUSE ME ...
I STILL CAN'T HEAR YOU! SHOUT IT FROM THE BOTTOM OF YOUR LUNGS!
OSU!

WHY AREN'T YOU DOING IT?
YOU'RE NOT GETTING OUT OF THIS FOR BEING A GIRL. CAN'T YOU SPEAK?
WHAT? HEY, I DON'T EVEN WANNA JOIN THE OUEN-

NO EX-CUSES!
YOU DO WHAT YOUR SENPAI TELLS YOU TO.
HMPH

DON'T GET COCKY WITH ME JUST 'CAUSE YOU'RE A THIRD YEAR.

I'M ACTUALLY 18, FOR YOUR INFORMATION.

AND I'LL BE 19 IN A MONTH!

YOU'VE GOT SOME NERVE, TALKING TO YOUR ELDERS LIKE THAT!

ひっ HURK

...?

OH, HEY!

USAMI!

YOU GOT SOME NEW MEMBERS, HUH?

TWO WHOLE NEW MEMBERS?

KITA-JIMA-SENSEI!

ACK...

SO KITAJIMA WAS THE OUENDAN'S CLUB SPONSOR, HUH?

HEY, IT'S THAT BLOND KID FROM THIS MORNING!

YOU'RE JOINING THE OUENDAN, HUH? GREAT!

WELL, COME ON IN, YOU TWO!

ポン PAT

ポン PAT

HEY!
WAIT!
NO!
I'M NOT JOINING THE OUENDAN, I'M GOING HOME!

...
...

GLANCE
チラ

STARE
じっ
?!

GAH!
IMAMURA!
LET'S CHEER TOGETHER!
DASH
I'LL BE WAITING FOR YOU!
WHAT DIFFERENCE DOES ONE GUY MAKE?
THIS IS THE SAME WORLD IT'S ALWAYS BEEN.

WELCOME HOME, KIN-CHAN!
HOW WAS SCHOOL? DID YOU MAKE ANY FRIENDS?
EXHAUSTED
ぐったり…
UHH, YEAH ...
THAT'S WONDERFUL! YOU CAN HAVE THEM OVER ANYTIME, OKAY?
I WAS WORRIED, SINCE WE JUST MOVED HERE AND ALL.
ARE YOU JOINING ANY CLUBS?
NAH.
I'M NOT.
I THINK I WANNA FIND A PART-TIME JOB.
THE OUENDAN SEEMS LIKE ONE GIANT PAIN IN THE ASS.
BUT...
...IF I DON'T JOIN NOW...

...IT'LL FALL APART.

RADIO CLUB

KIN-CHAAAAN!

IT'S MORNING!

SCHOOL FESTIVAL, 2009

CELEBRATION

KAGOSU MINAMI CELEBRATION

OUENDAN
2008
BASEBALL CHEERING
Supporting Kanan from the bleachers!

WHAT?
DAMN...
THE OUENDAN HAD PLENTY OF MEMBERS BEFORE I CAME HERE, HUH?
SHE MUST HAVE MESSED UP REALLY BAD SOME-HOW...

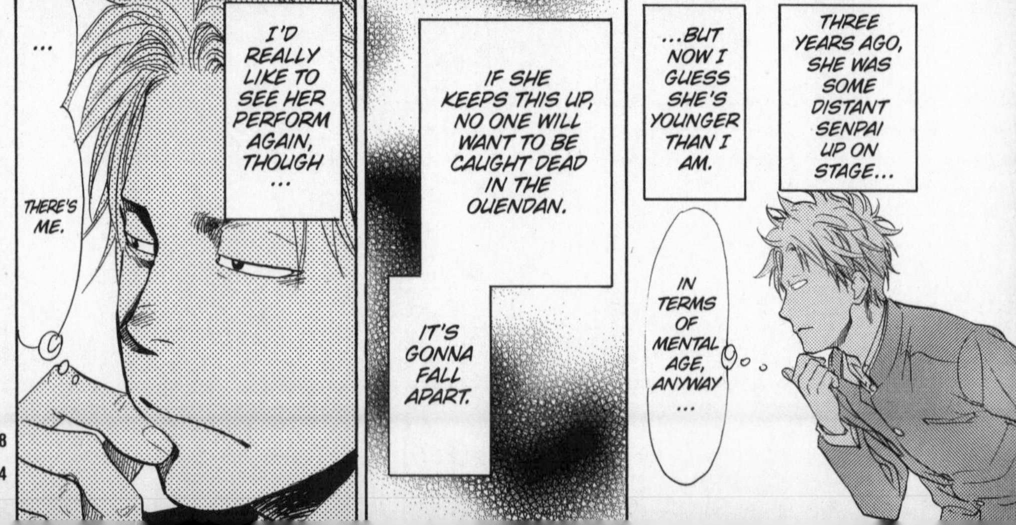

THREE YEARS AGO, SHE WAS SOME DISTANT SENPAI UP ON STAGE...
...BUT NOW I GUESS SHE'S YOUNGER THAN I AM.
IN TERMS OF MENTAL AGE, ANYWAY...
IF SHE KEEPS THIS UP, NO ONE WILL WANT TO BE CAUGHT DEAD IN THE OUENDAN.
IT'S GONNA FALL APART.
I'D REALLY LIKE TO SEE HER PERFORM AGAIN, THOUGH...
...
THERE'S ME.

THERE'S ME...

OUENDAN

MUNCH MUNCH

DUM DUDUM
?!
ACK!
GASP
CAPTAIN! I DIDN'T REALIZE YOU WERE HERE.
HEY!
WHO THE HELL IS MESSING WITH OUR TAIKO DRUMS?!
...
IMA-MURA?
YOU CAME BACK!
SO YOU'VE DECIDED YOU DO WANT TO BE PART OF THE OUENDAN, HUH? I APPRECIATE IT!
OUENDAN
RADIO CLUB
WELL ...
BEING PART OF IT IS ONE THING.
BUT I DON'T FEEL LIKE WORKING AT IT ALONE.

SO, LISTEN ...
...WE'VE GOTTA MAKE THE OUENDAN AS BIG AS IT USED TO BE.

IS THAT ANY WAY TO TALK TO YOUR SENPAI ?!

DON'T YOU DARE GET CUTE WITH ME!

S-SORRY...
FUNNY, THAT DIDN'T SOUND LIKE, "OSU"!
O-OSU.
I CAN'T HEAR YOU!
OSU!
WE'RE GONNA START BY WORKING ON YOUR VOICE PROJECTION!

OSU!
OSU!
HUH?
WHAT'S THAT?

THERE'S THIS STRANGE VOICE... I CAN'T TELL WHERE IT'S COMING FROM.
SCARY...
OSU!
OSU!
OSU!
YOU AIN'T DONE YET!
GIMME A HUNDRED MORE!
WHY DO THE GIRLS IN MY CLASS HAVE TO IGNORE ME?
GOD, I HAVEN'T EVEN SEEN IMAMURA AROUND...

4.
WE NEED YOU!

47!
48!
49!
50!
バターン
FWUMP

OKAY.
I'LL LET YOU LEAVE IT AT THAT FOR NOW.
THIS IS NOTHING COMPARED TO THE OUENDAN'S ACTUAL TRAINING REGIMEN, THOUGH.

...
ぜーはーぜーはー
WHEEZE
PANT
WHEEZE
PANT

GET IN THE CLUB ROOM.
AND DON'T FORGET THE MAGIC WORDS.

WHEEZE
PANT
WHEEZE
PANT
THIS IS A LOAD OF CRAP... WHY ME?
すぅ INHALE...
OSU!
EX-CUSE ME!
FWOO

KATHUNK
I'LL LET YOU OFF THE HOOK FOR RUNNING AWAY YESTERDAY.
YOU'VE DONE THE RIGHT THING BY COMING BACK.
WHOA...
IS THAT THE WEIGHT OF TRADITION I'M FEELING?
KABOSU MINAMI'S OUENDAN HAS A LONG HISTORY, LONGER THAN ANY OTHER IN THE PREFECTURE.

YOU GOT THAT?!
FROM HERE ON OUT, YOU MUST ALWAYS REMEMBER THAT YOU ARE A STUDENT OF KABOSU MINAMI HIGH.
YOU ARE TO CONDUCT YOURSELF IN A WAY THAT DOESN'T BRING SHAME TO THE OUENDAN. FURTHER...

SHE'S CUTE UNTIL SHE OPENS HER MOUTH. WHY'D SHE EVEN JOIN THE OUENDAN IN THE FIRST PLACE?

HEY! IMA-MURA!
POINT
ARE YOU LISTEN-ING?!
OH! YEAH. YEAH.
FUNNY, THAT DIDN'T SOUND LIKE, "OSU!"
SPEAK CLEAR-LY!
ACT WITH DISCI-PLINE AND INTEN-TION!

YOU ARE TO TRAIN UNTIL THESE THINGS BECOME INSTINCT.
THAT IS WHAT WE COMMIT OUR-SELVES TO EVERY TIME WE SAY, "OSU!"
SCRITCH
SCRITCH
DO I MAKE MY-SELF CLEAR?
WHAT DO YOU HAVE TO SAY FOR YOUR-SELF?
...

DO YOU HAVE *ANY* MOTIVATION TO BE A REAL MEMBER OF THE OUENDAN?!

OH.

NO, MA'AM.

NOT ONE BIT.

EX-CUSE ME?

I'LL BE FRANK. HOW MANY MEMBERS DO YOU HAVE RIGHT NOW?

ドスッ THUNK

DON'T SIT WITH-OUT ASK-ING!

CLUB POLICY STATES THAT YOU MAY ONLY SIT WITH THE PER-MISSION OF YOUR SENPAI.

WAS THAT GUY HOLDING THE FLAG THE ONLY ONE?

ARE THERE ANY MEMBERS AT LARGE OR ANY-THING LIKE THAT?

Doesn't look like it.

ガタッ CLATTER

OFFICIALLY SPEAKING, I'M THE ONLY MEMBER OF THE OUENDAN, BUT-

I BORROWED MIYAMOTO, THE FLAG-BEARER, FROM THE JUDO CLUB.

WHAT?
YOU'RE SERIOUSLY THE ONLY ONE?
YOU SAID YOU DIDN'T HAVE ***MANY*** MEMBERS, NOT THAT YOU DIDN'T HAVE ***ANY*** MEMBERS.
I SAW A DISPLAY ABOUT CLUB ACTIVITIES OUT IN THE HALLWAY, AND IT SURE LOOKED LIKE THE OUENDAN HAD PLENTY OF MEMBERS UNTIL LAST YEAR.
DID SOMETHING HAPPEN?
WHY IS IT JUST YOU NOW?
...

Y-YOU DON'T NEED TO KNOW, FIRST-YEAR!
AND WHAT'S WITH THE ATTITUDE?!

OHH, NO, NO.
I'M NOT TRYING TO TEASE.
JUST, WHAT IF NO ONE DECIDES TO JOIN?
I'M TALKING ABOUT AN ABSOLUTE WORST-CASE SCENARIO, Y'KNOW? IT SURE WOULD BE A SHAME IF THE OUENDAN FELL APART OR SOMETHING.
AND IT SEEMS LIKE MAYBE MORE PEOPLE WOULD JOIN IF YOU CHANGED HOW YOU DID THINGS A LITTLE BIT.
SO...

THERE'S STILL TIME.

I DON'T THINK IT'S TOO LATE TO CHANGE COURSE.

AND I WANNA GET TO SEE YOU CHEERING AGAIN, CAPTAIN.

FIRST,
YOU'RE GONNA HAVE TO LEARN HOW TO SPEAK MORE RESPECT-FULLY.
GOT THAT, IMA-MURA?

AGH...
OUENDA
OH!
IT'S IMA-MURA.
HEY, IMA-MURA!
I'VE BEEN LOOKING FOR YOU! WHERE WERE YOU?
へラ HURR
へラ HURR
へラ HURR
OSU!
むかあぁ... URRRRGH.
I THOUGHT THAT WAS SORT OF CUTE, DIDN'T I...
WHAT?!
YOU'RE JOINING THE OUENDAN, AFTER ALL?
SO IT'S ALL GOOD JUST 'CAUSE THE CAPTAIN IS CUTE, HUH? IS THAT IT, IMA-MURA?
YOU WERE NEVER EVEN IN A CLUB. DO YOU REALLY THINK YOU CAN DO THIS?!
NO, NO, NO.
IT'S NOT LIKE ...
...I WANT TO TAKE ON THE MANTLE OF CAPTAIN OR ANY-THING.

BUT SINCE WE'VE GONE THREE YEARS BACK IN TIME AND ALL,

I WANNA SEE IF I CAN CHANGE SOMETHING.

IT'D BE A DRAG JUST TO LIVE THE SAME CRAP ALL OVER AGAIN.

WHAT ARE YOU EVEN GONNA DO ABOUT THE OUENDAN, THOUGH?

WELL, I'VE GIVEN IT SOME THOUGHT...

NOW RECRUITING

IF YOU FEEL A CALLING, CONTACT USAMI IN CLASS 3-A

THE CAPTAIN HAS SUCH A PRETTY FACE, Y'KNOW?

IF SHE JUST PLAYED IT UP AND SOLD HERSELF AS A SCHOOL CELEBRITY, I BET SHE'D GET LOADS OF NEW MEMBERS.

BESIDES, SHE'D LOOK BETTER IN A CHEERLEADING OUTFIT THAN A BOY'S UNIFORM ANY DAY.

WAIT... BUT THE CHEERLEADERS-

...

RRRIP

ALL RIGHT!

LET'S PUT OPERATION CELEBRITY INTO ACTION!

?!

NOW RECRUITING

WE NEED YOU & YOUR POWER!

WE NEED YOU TO LEND US YOUR STRENGTH!

お話を聞きたい！

加保須南を応援したい！

という1年生は、すぐに！

3年A組 団長 宇佐美 良子 まで

BAM!

バン!!

WHAT'S THIS ALL ABOUT?

THE OUEN-DAN?

OH YEAH. THIS MUST BE THE WORK OF THAT CAPTAIN OF THEIRS.

HEY!
THERE SHE IS!
HER SCHOOL UNIFORM LOOKS MORE LIKE A COSTUME ON HER THAN THAT OUENDAN GET-UP DOES.
HAHA
?
NOW RECRUITING
WE NEED YOU TO LEND US YOUR STRENGTH!
WE NEED YOU & YOUR POWER!

KITAJIMA-SENSEI, WOULD YOU PLEASE EXPLAIN THESE POSTERS TO ME?!

HI THERE, USAMI.

OH, YOU TORE THE POSTERS DOWN, HUH? THAT'S A SHAME.

IMAMURA CAME TO ME DURING BREAK SAYING HE WANTED A PICTURE OF YOU TO MAKE THEM WITH.

PANT PANT

I WAS PRETTY IMPRESSED. HE SAT RIGHT DOWN AT THE COMPUTER AND WHIPPED UP A POSTER ON THE SPOT. THAT BOY'S GOT SOME SKILLS!

TAP TAP TAP

Whoa! You're fast.

TAP TAP

IMA-MURA DID THIS?

PERSONALLY, I DO THINK IT'S CUTE, BUT THERE'S SOMETHING ABOUT IT...

...

CRUMPLE

FWUMP
ドサ…
THAT WAS EXHAUSTING!
BUT I PUT THEM ALL UP!
THEY MIGHT NOT STAY UP LONG, THOUGH, SINCE YOU DIDN'T GET PERMISSION TO POST THEM.
GREAT, THANKS.
I'M SURE IT'LL BE FINE. EVEN JUST A DAY OF ADVERTISING WILL HELP WORD GET AROUND. IT'S BETTER THAN NOTHING.

AND Y'KNOW WHAT ELSE? I WAS THINKING, AND I REMEMBERED HOW MANY DORKS SPENT THEIR THREE YEARS IN THOSE DULL-ASS CULTURAL CLUBS, OR JUST HANGING AROUND WITH THEIR PALS. WE SHOULD TRY TO GET ALL OF THEM ON BOARD.
WITH HOW BOSSY THE CAPTAIN IS, I'M SURE SHE CAN SCARE ONE OR TWO OF THEM INTO STICKING AROUND.

FUJIEDA, YOU HAVE A LOT OF FRIENDS, DON'T YOU?
ISN'T THERE ANYONE YOU COULD INVITE TO JOIN THE OUENDAN?
FLINCH
びくっ
UH …
OH YEAH …
ガラ…
SLIDE
IMAMURA.
CAPTAIN.

LOOK AT THIS.

NOW RECRUITING

EX-PLAIN.

ISN'T IT GREAT?

I MEAN, PEOPLE AREN'T REALLY INTERESTED IN THE OUENDAN THESE DAYS, 'CAUSE THEY THINK IT'S TOO OLD-FASHIONED OR HARDCORE, RIGHT?

IT'S NOT LIKE IT CAN HELP YOU GET INTO COLLEGE, EITHER, SO WHO'D WANNA JOIN JUST TO GET PUT THROUGH BOOT CAMP?
EVI-DENTLY, NO-BODY.

AND OUR SCHOOL ISN'T EXACTLY THE BEST AT ATHLETICS, SO IT DOESN'T EVEN GIVE YOU THE CHANCE TO SEE THE NATIONAL STADIUM OR GO TO THE BASEBALL CHAMPIONSHIPS.

YOU CAN PUT IN AS MUCH WORK AS YOU WANT, CAPTAIN, BUT NOTHING'S GONNA CHANGE AS LONG AS YOU'RE ON YOUR OWN.

THAT'S WHAT GOT ME THINKING: YOU SHOULD MAKE THE OUENDAN SEEM MORE FUN, AND TURN HAVING A GIRL CAPTAIN INTO A SELLING POINT.
Uh-huh.
OH!
AND I WAS SAYING EARLIER, INSTEAD OF THAT BOY'S UNIFORM,
WHY DON'T YOU WEAR A CHEER-LEADING OUTFIT?
THAT WOULD GO OVER *WAY* BET-
DRIP
DRIP

HUH ?

WHAT-EVER.
NEVER SET FOOT IN MY CLUB ROOM AGAIN.

WELP ...

DID I SAY SOMETHING WRONG?

OH, GOD! ARE YOU *THAT* OBLIVIOUS?

OF COURSE, I MEAN, YOU *ARE* RIGHT, IMAMURA.

MAYBE IT'S JUST TIME FOR THE OUENDAN TO FADE AWAY.

HEY, ONCE THERE WAS NO MORE OUENDAN, WHO DID THE CHEERING FOR OUR SCHOOL'S SPORTS TEAMS?
WAIT, YOU DON'T REMEMBER?

HEY, USAMI-SAN.
FLINCH
TAKING THOSE POSTERS DOWN, HUH? THAT'S A SHAME.

SO,
THINK YOU'RE GONNA FIND ANY MEMBERS IN TIME FOR OUR INTER-CLUB TRAINING SESH?
KANAN
ABE-SAN...
THE OUENDAN GOT TAKEN OVER BY THE CHEER-LEADING CLUB.
?!

5. CHEERLEADER RAPID FIRE

I'VE BEEN TRYING TO TELL YOU, USAMI-SAN.

YOU'RE SO PRETTY, YOU'D GET A LOT OF BOYS JOINING UP, FOR SURE.

WHEN I SAW THESE POSTERS, I THOUGHT YOU'D FINALLY COME AROUND.

WHY NOT LEAVE THEM UP?

THIS IS THE UNAUTHORIZED WORK OF MY NEWEST MEMBER.

TEAR

WAIT!

OH MY GOD. YOU HAVE A NEW MEMBER?

A GUY OR A GIRL?

A- A GUY.

OH, A GUY, HUH?

I HOPE THAT WORKS OUT.

I MEAN, HE'S NOT ANOTHER ONE WHO'S JUST GONNA QUIT ON YOU, RIGHT?

ULP ...

I DON'T MEAN TO DISCOURAGE YOU, USAMI-SAN.

I REALLY HOPE THE OUENDAN CAN CHEER WITH US. I'M JUST WORRIED.

I MEAN, THE CHEERLEADING CLUB DOES HAVE WAY MORE MEMBERS, AFTER ALL.

IF YOU NEED HELP WITH ANYTHING AT ALL, FEEL FREE TO TALK TO ME, OKAY?

ANYWAY,

I'LL SEE YOU NEXT WEEK AT THE INTERCLUB TRAINING SESSION. ♥

DON'T SWEAT IT IF YOU CAN'T GET TOGETHER THE MEMBERS YOU'LL NEED.

I'LL MAKE SURE WE'RE READY TO PERFORM WITH OR WITHOUT YOU.

BAM BAM BAM BAM

HEY, CAPTAIN!

FLINCH

CHACK CHACK KACHAK

BAM BAM

BAM

YOU IN THERE?

I'M SORRY ABOUT EARLIER.

BAM

PLEASE OPEN THE DOOR.

OUENDAN

BAM

BAM

GOD,

YOU DO NOT SOUND LIKE YOU MEAN THAT.

BAM

I HEARD ABOUT THE STUFF WITH THE CHEER-LEADING CLUB.
BAM BAM ドンドン
THEY'VE JUST ABOUT TAKEN THE OUENDAN'S PLACE DUE TO YOUR LACK OF MEMBERS, RIGHT?
BAM ドン
BAM ドン
I'M SORRY FOR SAYING YOU SHOULD WEAR A CHEERLEADING OUTFIT OR WHATEVER.
SLIDE
WHOA.
DIDN'T I TELL YOU...
...NEVER TO SET FOOT IN HERE AGAIN?
SERI-OUSLY?
SLIIIDE
?!
THMP

HEY, I SAID I'M SORRY ABOUT HOW I PUT THINGS EARLIER,

DIDN'T I?

YOU NEED ALL THE HELP YOU CAN GET RIGHT NOW!

I KNOW I SAID YOU SHOULD PLAY UP YOUR GENDER AND THAT YOU'RE BEHIND THE TIMES...

...AND I MEAN, I GUESS I STILL THINK SO, BUT Y'KNOW.

YOU'RE JUST TOO STUBBORN, CAPTAIN. YOU'VE GOTTA-

THWUNK

I'M GONNA MAKE THIS CLUB GROW MY OWN WAY. JUST YOU WATCH.
YOU'RE USELESS TO ME IF YOU CAN'T HANDLE HOW WE DO THINGS IN THE OUENDAN.
NOW GET OUT OF HERE, YOU LITTLE PUNK!
SHMP
WELL, WHAT NOW?
WE'RE RIGHT BACK WHERE WE STARTED.

DAMN IT!

WHAT THE HELL? I WAS TRYING TO BE A NICE GUY, SINCE SHE WAS CRYING AND ALL.

NO WAY ANYONE'S GONNA JOIN HER CLUB IF SHE KEEPS THAT UP.

THEN WHY DON'T YOU JUST LEAVE HER ALONE?

EVENTUALLY, THE CAPTAIN WILL STEP DOWN, AND THAT'LL BE THE END OF THAT.

WHAT'S THE BIG DEAL?

DRIP

DRIP

...
THROB THROB
BEFORE WE WENT BACK IN TIME, THE CHEERLEADERS WERE DOING AS GOOD A JOB AS THE OUENDAN EVER DID, SO WHO CARES?

WE'RE DOING THE WHOLE ROUTINE FROM THE BEGIN-NING THIS TIME.
ONE, TWO, THREE, AND GO!

Go Fight!
WHOA ...
Go Fight!
THERE ARE SO MANY OF THEM ...
THEY DO WELL IN COMPETITIONS, SO IT'S A POPULAR CLUB.
AND A ONE-MEMBER OUENDAN ISN'T ENOUGH TO CHEER ON ALL A SCHOOL'S TEAMS,
SO IT'S PRETTY COMMON FOR THAT STUFF TO JUST BE PART OF THE CHEERLEADING CLUB.
MHMM ...
HURR
HURR
URRGH
MEN! FIGURES YOU ALL JUST WANT SOME GIRL WHO LOOKS LIKE SHE'D DATE THE QUARTERBACK ON AN AMERICAN SITCOM!
YOU'RE THE WORST.
COME AGAIN?
What are you talking about?

HEY, YOU TWO!
WHO ARE YOU?
?!
?
UH ...
WELL ...
TH-
THIS GUY'S FROM THE OUENDAN AND WANTED TO WATCH YOU PRACTICE!
HE'S THEIR NEWEST MEMBER.
RIGHT ?
HEY.
OH, I SEE.
I GUESS WE WILL BE TRAINING TOGETHER NEXT WEEK.
HUH ?
WHAT DO YOU MEAN ?
YOU HAVEN'T HEARD ?

OUR ANNUAL INTERLEAGUE BASEBALL GAME IS RIGHT AROUND THE CORNER.

EVERY YEAR, THE CHEER-LEADING CLUB, THE OUENDAN, AND THE BASEBALL CLUB'S BENCHERS WORK TOGETHER TO CHEER OUR TEAM ON, SO WE'LL BE TRAINING FOR THAT NEXT WEEK.

OH ...

ANYWAY, I'M GLAD TO SEE A BOY LIKE YOU HAS JOINED THE OUENDAN!

THINGS HAVEN'T BEEN EASY WITH THE ONLY MEMBER BEING THAT CAPTAIN OF YOURS.

HEY, COACH.

LET'S HURRY UP AND GET BACK TO PRACTICE.

YOU GUYS STICK AROUND AND WATCH.

RIGHT!

OKAY.

DUM
DUM
DUM
DUM
DADUM
DAMN ...

Y'KNOW
...
IF THE CAPTAIN WERE HERE...

I'll be just fine on my own!!
THE CLUBS WILL BE TRAINING TOGETHER NEXT WEEK, HUH?
Ugh, Imamura! You were just trying to decide which of them you like best, weren't you? That's gross, you jerk!
I SORT OF DOUBT ANYONE BESIDES ME WILL HAVE JOINED THE OUENDAN BY THEN ...

OH ...

I'M KIN-ICHIRO IMA-MURA.

WELL, HI.

I'M THE CHEER CAPTAIN HERE, TAMAKI ABE.

NICE TO MEET YOU. ♥

YEAH ...

IT'S COOL THAT A GUY LIKE YOU JOINED ALL ON YOUR OWN.

I'm surprised!

THEN AGAIN,

I BET USAMI-SAN WAS A MOTIVATING FACTOR, HUH?

COME ON, YOU KNOW WHAT I MEAN.

HUH?

UH-OH.

I knew it.

giggle giggle

FIG-URES.

SHE'S SO PRETTY, AFTER ALL!

IS THAT WHAT THEY THINK OF ME?

WHAT A PAIN IN THE ASS ...

GOTTA GO.

WHAT. IS. HIS. PROB-LEM?!

THAT'S SOME NERVE FOR A FIRST-YEAR!

THAT JERK!

THINK HE'S IN A GANG?

WHO KNOWS?

AND WHY'D HE BRING THAT GIRL?

UGH, WHY'D A CREEP LIKE HIM HAVE TO JOIN THE OUENDAN?

OH GOD, AT THIS RATE, HE'LL BE THEIR NEXT CAPTAIN!

TWIRL

CHEERING WITH USAMI'S BAD ENOUGH!

You just use your looks to win favor.

It disgusts me.

Heh heh heh heh heh... What a bunch of sluts.

JUST THE THOUGHT OF HAVING TO WORK WITH HIM MAKES ME WANNA GAG!

I'M IN THE SAME CLASS AS HIM.

HE'S SUCH A LONER IT'S SCARY.

TWITCH

← One of the new girls

THERE'S NO WAY!

I VOTE NO!

EW, NO!

YOU'RE IN THE SAME CLASS AS HIM?!
くるっ
TWIRL
YEAH ...
YOU POOR THING ...
?

AGH,
I DON'T THINK I'VE EVER TALKED TO GIRLS AS MUCH AS I JUST DID.
YOU CAN HAVE YOUR GIRL-FRIEND OVER ANYTIME, SWEETIE!
NO ...
I THINK EVERY SINGLE GIRL I TALKED TO TODAY HATES ME.
DIIING
DAAAANG
DOOOONG
DOOOONG
I NEED TO FIND THE CAP-TAIN.
MAYBE SHE'S IN THE WEST BUILD-ING?
CLATTER
I'M HUN-GRY!
LET'S EAT TOGETH-ER!

I GUESS...
...I'LL GO APOLOGIZE AGAIN.
...
HEY. IMAMURA-KUN.
PAT
SMILE
HUH?
WHO'S THIS?
REMEMBER ME?
I WAS ONE OF THE CHEERLEADERS YOU SAW YESTERDAY.
BWA?
OHHH, OKAY.
WHAT IS IT?

LET'S HAVE LUNCH TOGETHER.
WHAT?
HEY, CAN IMAMURA JOIN US?
HE SAYS HE'S ALL ALONE.
SURE!
WHAT THE HELL IS THIS ALL ABOUT ?!

6. TROUBLEMAKER?

LET'S HAVE LUNCH TOGETHER.

OH ...

DO YOU ALREADY HAVE PLANS WITH SOMEONE ELSE?

NO ...
I GUESS I DON'T ...

GREAT.
BY THE WAY, YOU DON'T MIND IF MY FRIENDS JOIN US, DO YOU?
OH.
NO.
WHY NOT ...
IN MY THREE YEARS OF HIGH SCHOOL, NOT ONCE DID I EVER HAVE "PLANS" WITH ANYONE.

LUCKILY, IT DIDN'T TAKE LONG AFTER I STARTED SCHOOL HERE BEFORE I FOUND AN ABANDONED CORNER OF CAMPUS I COULD ESCAPE TO.
FOR THREE YEARS, I'D GO THERE ALL BY MYSELF TO DO STUFF LIKE EAT LUNCH AND CUT CLASS.

I NEVER MADE ANY FRIENDS, AND I NEVER TRIED TO, EITHER.
NO ONE EVER TALKED TO ME. I WAS PRACTICALLY INVISIBLE...

AND YET HERE I AM, HAVING LUNCH IN THE CLASS-ROOM FOR THE FIRST TIME WITH THREE GIRLS.
GIVE ME A BREAK!
...

I GUESS WE HAVEN'T REALLY MET, HUH?

MY NAME'S REO SHIBATA.

OH, AND I'M REO'S FRIEND FROM CRAM SCHOOL, EMA YAMANOUCHI.

Nice to meet ya.

EMA AND I WENT TO THE SAME MIDDLE SCHOOL. THE NAME'S CHIE YAMANE.

UHHHHH...
SCRITCH
SCRITCH
KIN-ICHIRO IMAMURA.
IS...
MY NAME.

I'D HAVE BEEN BETTER OFF EATING ALONE.
THIS IS AWKWARD!
NOM NOM NOM

WHISPER WHISPER
WHISPER WHISPER
WHISPER WHISPER
WERE WE IN THE SAME CLASS OUR FIRST YEAR?
SHE DOESN'T SEEM FAMILIAR...
REO SHIBATA...
REO...
WAIT.
THAT REO?

OH! I REMEMBER NOW!
REO SHIBATA!
FLINCH
HUH?
WHAT?

JUST,
I REMEMBER YOUR NAME.
YOU HAD SUCH GOOD GRADES. I'D ALWAYS SEE YOUR NAME NEAR THE TOP OF THE CHART.
I THOUGHT IT SOUNDED FANCY.
HEY!
YOU DO KNOW HER.
REO'S GOT A REPUTATION FOR BEING ONE OF THE SMART KIDS AT OUR CRAM SCHOOL, TOO.
HEY, CUT IT OUT.

REO SHIBATA. SHE HAD THE BEST GRADES OUT OF ALL THE GIRLS IN OUR YEAR.

I'M PRETTY SURE SHE ENDED UP GETTING INTO SOME SUPER-PRESTIGIOUS COLLEGE.

Y'KNOW, THOUGH, I'M SURPRISED YOU JOINED THE CHEERLEADING CLUB, REO.

YOU WERE JUST STUDY, STUDY, STUDY ALL THROUGH MIDDLE SCHOOL, WEREN'T YOU?

OH, YOU DIDN'T DO ANY SPORTS, REO?

WELL, NO.

JUST...

DOING NOTHING BUT STUDYING FOR THREE YEARS DIDN'T SOUND FUN...

...SO I THOUGHT I'D TRY SOMETHING TOTALLY DIFFERENT.

FIDGET FIDGET

いじいじ

WOW.

ARE YOU SURE A QUIET GIRL LIKE YOU WILL BE ABLE TO FIT IN WITH THOSE CHEERLEADERS, SHIBATA-SAN?

GULP

NOT A PROBLEM!

I'LL BE FINE!

HMM...

I HOPE SO.

...

HEY, IMAMURA.

WHY'D YOU GO BLOND?

WHAT'S IT TO YOU?

I'VE BEEN WONDERING ABOUT THAT, TOO.

...

WELL, I HEARD THIS SCHOOL'S DRESS CODE DIDN'T HAVE ANY RESTRICTIONS ABOUT YOUR HAIR.

SO I WENT TO MY USUAL STYLIST BEFORE I MOVED HERE AND GOT A LITTLE CARRIED AWAY.

HE DID THIS TO ME WHILE I WAS SLEEPING.

What do you think?

THAT'S IT?
IT'S NOT, LIKE, A STATEMENT OR SOMETHING?
NOD
NOD

SER-
IOUSLY?
OH MY
GOD!
DAMN
!
SO
YOU'RE
NOT IN A
GANG?
NO,
I'M NOT
IN A
GANG!
THAT'S
FUNNY
!
I COULD'VE
SWORN
HE WAS
TRYING TO
BE A REBEL
OR SOME-
THING!
WAIT,
WAIT.
SO...
WHY DO
YOU SHAVE
YOUR EYE-
BROWS?
I DON'T.
THEY'RE
JUST
THIN. MY
GRANDMA
DOESN'T
HAVE ANY,
EITHER.
YOU'RE A
GRAND-
MA'S
BOY!
THAT'S
HILAR-
IOUS!
AH
HA
HA
HA
HA
HEY,
YOU'RE
GOING
OVER-
BOARD.
YOU
USED
TO
LIVE
IN
TOKYO,
RIGHT
?
WHAT
PART?
WHAT
KIND
OF
MUSIC
DO YOU
LISTEN
TO?
GUH.
SO MUCH
FOR BEING
TAKEN
SERIOUSLY.

JEALOUSY
LURK!!
AH HA HA HA HA HA
WHAT'S WITH THAT?
I MEAN, I JUST—
...
This tea tastes awful!
Try it! It's really bad!
Why would I do that?!
Hey.
I want some.
CLENCH
Y'KNOW,
I JUST THOUGHT YOU'D BE WAY SCARIER, IMAMURA.
ME, TOO.

WELL, HERE'S WHAT'S GOT ME.
I'VE NEVER EATEN LUNCH IN THE CLASSROOM BEFORE.
AND I DON'T HAVE ANY FRIENDS.
SO I HAVE NO IDEA WHY WE'RE DOING THIS.

HUSH...
WHOA.
DON'T GET ALL QUIET ON ME.

GOD, YOU REALLY DON'T HAVE ANY FRIENDS?
That's creepy!
WHAT ABOUT THAT GIRL YOU WERE WITH YESTER-DAY?

OH, HER?
JERK!
STUPID!
I MEAN... WE'RE NOT EXACTLY FRIENDS. I DON'T THINK. WE JUST KNOW EACH OTHER.

...
PHEW...

WELL ...
YOU'RE IN THE OUENDAN, THOUGH.
WHAT ABOUT YOUR CAP-TAIN?

THE CAPTAIN ...
SORT OF ...
...HATES ME RIGHT NOW.
SHE TOLD ME NEVER TO SET FOOT IN THE CLUB ROOM AGAIN.

HUH ?
SLIDE

OSU!
I'M USAMI, CAPTAIN OF THE OUENDAN.
FIRST-YEARS, I NEED TO SPEAK WITH YOU!
?!
RIGHT NOW, I'M GOING FROM CLASS TO CLASS SEEKING OUT NEW RECRUITS FOR THE OUENDAN.
DO I HAVE ANY VOLUN-TEERS ?!

God, what's this all about?
She's scary!
IF YOU'RE UNCERTAIN, I'LL ALLOW YOU TO JOIN ON A TENTATIVE BASIS!
YOU MAY WAIT UNTIL YOU HAVE A BETTER UNDER-STANDING OF THE OUENDAN'S ACTIVITIES BEFORE MAKING YOUR FINAL DECISION.

HEY, CAPTAIN.
CLATTER
SO ... HOW ABOUT ME?

I'M IN SEARCH OF RECRUITS WHO ARE PREPARED TO JOIN ME IN MAINTAINING THE SPIRIT AND TRADITIONS OF THE OUENDAN!

THOSE OF YOU WHO JUST WANT TO FLIRT WITH GIRLS OVER LUNCH CAN STAY HOME!

I'LL BE TRAINING IN FRONT OF THE SCHOOL GATES ONCE CLASSES ARE OVER.

COME SEE FOR YOURSELVES ON YOUR WAY OUT.

THAT IS ALL!

SLIDE

OSU!!

CHATTER CHATTER

...

SHE MUST...

...HATE ME EVEN MORE NOW.

I SURE BLEW THAT...

I GUESS...

...I'LL GO SEE THE CAPTAIN.

HEY, IMAMURA.

LISTEN.

REO WANTS TO-

GAAAAH!

I MEAN, ARE YOU SURE?

IT'S FINE! JUST STOP. STOP IT.

WELL, LATER THEN!

SEE YOU TOMORROW!

BYE-BYE!

......

...?

BYE...

WHAT THE HELL?

INSIDE SHOES O

I WANT ...

...TO WALK HOME WITH YOU.

OH.
I'M ACTUALLY GOING TO SEE THE CAPTAIN.
HURK
SEE YA.
HEY!
NO!
UHH...
GRAB
W- WAIT UP!
THERE'S SOME-THING I WANT TO TELL YOU.

HEY, SHE'S NOT TOO BAD.
AND SHE WAS SO HESITANT AT FIRST.
RIGHT?
SHE SEEMS LIKE SHE LIKES IMAMURA SORT OF A LOT, DOESN'T SHE?
TEE-HEE!
YOU CAN MAKE ANY BOY INTO YOUR TOY IF YOU DO AS I TELL YOU.

WE WERE BORN AS GIRLS ...
...SO WE HAVE TO BECOME TIGERS.
REO.
I WANT YOU TO STEAL HIS HEART FROM THE OUENDAN'S CAPTAIN FOR ME, OKAY?

AFTER ALL, IT'S DEFINITELY IN HIS BEST INTEREST NOT TO JOIN THAT SILLY LITTLE CLUB OF HERS.

7. WE WANT TO CHEER WITH YOU!

offers
of.

SCHOOL

Stude
in
class
(main
building

LING SCHOOL LIFE
ch day is divided into five periods.
when we finish up. After
independent

CAPTAIN ABE,
WHAT ADVICE DID YOU GIVE HER ABOUT SEDUCING IMAMURA, ANYWAY?
OH, IT WAS KID STUFF.
ANY OF YOU GIRLS COULD PULL IT OFF.

GET SUGGESTIVE WITH YOUR TARGET WHEN HE DOESN'T EXPECT IT,

AND THEN LEAVE HIM WANTING MORE.

RINSE AND REPEAT.

HE'LL BE LIKE, "HUH? WHY IS SHE ACTING THAT WAY TOWARDS ME?"

KEEP THAT UP, AND SOON ENOUGH YOU'LL HAVE HIM WRAPPED AROUND YOUR LITTLE FINGER. THAT'S ALL.

OF COURSE, YOU HAVE TO STRIKE THE RIGHT BALANCE.

BUT REO-CHAN'S SMART. I THINK SHE CAN FIGURE IT OUT.

I MEAN, WE'RE TALKING *IMAMURA* HERE, THE GUY WITH NO FRIENDS.

I DOUBT HE CAN RESIST.

UHH ...
HEY ... IMA-MURA-KUN?
SWEEP
ACK!
?!
UGH, WHY IS SHE ACTING THIS WAY TOWARDS ME?
SHE WANTS TO WALK HOME WITH ME?
THERE'S SOME-THING SHE WANTS TO TELL ME?
IMA-MURA-KUN?

DON'T TAKE ME FOR A FOOL. I SPENT MY ENTIRE HIGH SCHOOL CAREER IN ISOLATION.
WHY ME?
WE JUST MET!
THIS HAS GOT TO BE PART OF SOME SCHEME!
SHATTER
SEEMS PRETTY WEIRD, DON'T YOU THINK?
HEY, IMA-MURA-KUN.
I'M SORRY.
IMA-MURA-KUN? DID I SAY SOME-THING WRONG?
YOU'RE A SMART GIRL, SHIBATA-SAN.
WHAT DO YOU HAVE TO GAIN FROM TALKING TO AN IDIOT LIKE ME?
GLANCE
CAP-TAIN ...

SHUDDER
UGH.
UH, COME ON?
GO GET HIM!
OF COURSE ...
...IT'S NOT LIKE WE DON'T HAVE A PLAN B.
HOORAY!
HOORAY!
MI NA O MI!

HEY! HEY!
MI-NA-MI!
NOW RECRUITING!

KANAAAN!
GO!
GO, TEAM!
GOOO!
OH GOD...

EVERYONE'S JUST PRETENDING SHE'S NOT THERE.
RECRUITING LIKE THAT ISN'T GONNA GET ANYONE TO JOIN.

STAY HOME!!
SHE'LL PROBABLY JUST YELL AT ME AGAIN IF I TRY TO TALK TO HER...
Ugh...

HEY ...
EX-CUSE ME.

WHAT IS IT?

WELL ...
Y'SEE, I...

I WAS PRETTY MOVED BY YOUR PER-FORMANCE AT THE ENTRANCE CEREMONY.
I'VE BEEN TOO EMBAR-RASSED TO COME TALK TO YOU ABOUT IT.

BUT ...

...I WANT TO JOIN THE OUENDAN!

HUH?!

ALSO ...

...MY FRIENDS SEEM INTER-ESTED, TOO.
YOUR CHEERING AT THE ENTRANCE CEREMONY REALLY TOUCHED MY HEART!
YOU'RE SO COOL!
I WANNA CHEER LIKE THAT!
HUH ...?
HMM ?
UH ...
I'D LIKE TO JOIN, TOO.
HEY.
THEY'RE STILL RECRUIT-ING FOR THE OUENDAN.
REALLY ?!
STOMP
STOMP
STOMP
YEEAH!!
CAP-TAIN!
WE WANT TO CHEER WITH YOU!

WHAT ...
IS THIS SOME KIND OF PRANK?!
HRGH
THERE'S GOT TO BE SOME-THING WEIRD GOING ON HERE!
...
YEEEEAH
CAP-TAIN!
WE'RE WITH YOU!
CAP-TAIN!
LET'S DO OUR BEST!

OSU!
YOU GUYS... THANK YOU! THANK YOU SO MUCH!

URRRGH

THE HELL WITH THIS!
バッ
FWIP
STOMP
ズン
STOMP
STOMP
OH.
HEY, IMAMURA-KUN.
DO YOU LEAVE FROM THE BACK GATE?
MAYBE I COULD HEAD OVER THERE WITH YOU.

SO…
…THERE WASN'T EVEN ANY POINT IN PUTTING IN ALL THAT EFFORT, HUH?
PANT
PANT
PANT
RUSTLE
RUSTLE
IMA-MURA-KUN.
DID YOU WANT TO JOIN THE OUENDAN THAT BADLY?
PANT
PANT
TMP
TMP
NOPE.
NOT REAL-LY.
PANT
DON'T YOU LIKE CHEER-ING, THOUGH?
PANT
PANT!
THEN…
YOU MUST'VE REALLY LIKED THE CAPTAIN, HUH?
NOT REAL-LY.
I DON'T CARE ABOUT SPORTS, ANYWAY.
OKAY! COME ON!
KATING
PANT
PANT
FWOOO

NO,
I DON'T LIKE HER!
I JUST ...
... THOUGHT SHE NEEDED ME.
BUT I WAS WRONG.

HUH?

WHAT DO YOU MEAN, "GOOD"?

NEVER MIND.

SHAKE ぶんっぶんっ SHAKE

BYE NOW.

学校に用事がない方の
立ち入りはできません

I'LL SEE YOU TOMORROW.

UH,

YEAH, BYE.

OH!

REMEMBER HOW CHIE-CHAN WANTED YOU TO LEND HER A CD?

LEND ME ONE, TOO, OKAY?

AND I'LL BRING SOMETHING FOR YOU TO BORROW.

I— I'M BACK.
HEY THERE.
HMM.
YOU MAY BE BOOK SMART, REO-CHAN, BUT I GUESS ROMANCE ISN'T EASY WHEN YOU DON'T HAVE ANY EXPERIENCE, HUH?
YOU COULD'VE AT LEAST HELD HANDS WITH HIM.
GRR

I'M NOT SO SURE.
WOULDN'T IT SEEM UNNATURAL TO DO THAT OUT OF NOWHERE WITH A BOY I ONLY JUST MET IN THE LAST DAY OR TWO?
IMA-MURA-KUN WAS REALLY SUS-PICIOUS OF ME.

THAT'S 'CAUSE YOU WERE ACTING ALL NERVOUS, HUN.
HAVE A LITTLE CONFIDENCE. USE YOUR FEMININE WILES ON HIM.
LIFT
HE'S GOTTA HAVE A THING FOR YOU, SINCE YOU HAVE THE SAME HAIRCUT AS CAPTAIN USAMI AND ALL. I GUARANTEE IT.
'KAY?

AND HEY, WE ALL MADE GOOD USE OF OUR FEMININE WILES TO PLANT THOSE BOYS IN THE OUENDAN!
RIGHT?
MY DEAR LITTLE FIRST-YEARS?
RIGHT!

HUH?!
SO... YOU GUYS MADE THAT HAPPEN?
What the hell?
Captain!
Hey, Captain!
Right on, Captain!
IT REALLY DID SEEM STAGED...

OH, HEY.
OSU!
OSU!
OSU!
SOUNDS LIKE USAMI'S STARTED PRACTICE.
THOSE BOYS ARE GONNA WORK THEIR BUTTS OFF FOR HER UNTIL THE BIG DAY...
OSU!
LOUDER!
OSU!
OSU!
YOU AREN'T DONE YET!

...AND THEN THEY'LL QUIT ALL AT ONCE RIGHT BEFORE OUR INTERCLUB TRAINING.
I CAN'T WAIT TO SEE THE LOOK ON USAMI'S FACE! ☆
THAT'S WHY YOU'VE GOTTA SEE TO IT THAT IMAMURA DOESN'T REJOIN THE OUENDAN, REO-CHAN.
HE SEEMS JUST SHARP ENOUGH TO GET IN OUR WAY.

ANY-WAY!
HOW'S ABOUT WE PUT THE FINISHING TOUCHES ON THE NO-OUENDAN VERSION OF OUR BASEBALL CHEERS?
YEAH!
WE CHEER-LEADERS HAVE GOTTA SHOW KANAN HIGH THE MEANING OF PEP!
MINAMIIII!
GO, TEAM, GOooo!
GO, TEAM, GOooo!
EVERYBODY!
GO, TEAM, GOooo!
...
I SEE ...

8. ORDINARY WORLD: REALM OF BOREDOM

GOOD MORNING!
MORNING.

IT'S BEEN A FEW DAYS NOW...
...SINCE I WENT THREE YEARS BACK IN TIME TO THE DAY OF MY ENTRANCE CEREMONY.
I'm tired.

OH, HEY.
GOOD MORNING, IMAMURA-KUN!
MORNING!
MORNING...
WHOA, YOU LOOK AWFUL.
YOU MUST HAVE BEEN UP LATE, HUH?
WOBBLE
I'VE GOT THE GOODS.
OOH, REALLY?
AW YEAH, I'M READY FOR THIS.
RUSTLE

WELL, THESE SONGS ARE SOME OF THIS BAND'S BETTER ONES, BUT THIS NEXT TRACK IS THE ONE THAT'S REALLY GONNA MAKE THEM BIG.

I THINK YOU GIRLS WOULD PROBABLY LIKE IT.

TAP

TAP

TAP

NOW, ABOUT THAT BAND I LENT YOU LAST WEEK.

THEY'RE GONNA BREAK UP OVER SOME INFIGHTING PRETTY SOON, SO YOU MIGHT WANNA GO TO ONE OF THEIR CONCERTS WHILE YOU STILL CAN.

OH, AND THIS MANGA? IT'S SORT OF AIMED AT NERDS, BUT THE MOVIE THEY MADE OUT OF IT WAS GENERALLY PRETTY WELL RECEIVED.

IT'S ALMOST LIKE HE KNOWS THE FUTURE.
I DON'T FREAKIN' KNOW THE FUTURE!
ROAR
GASP
HUSH....
OH... S-SORRY...
NOW THERE ARE THREE PEOPLE I CAN ACTUALLY TALK TO IN MY CLASS...
...BUT THIS DAILY ROUTINE ISN'T ANY LESS BORING THAN IT WAS THREE YEARS AGO.
AND DON'T GET ME STARTED ON THE AGONY OF RETAKING CLASSES I'VE ALREADY BEEN THROUGH...
It's exasperating.
HEY! IMAMURA!
NOW COME SOLVE THIS PROBLEM!
YOU HAVE TO PAY ATTENTION!

CLATTER
...FINE.
WE HAVEN'T EVEN COVERED THIS STUFF YET, THOUGH.
THIS TEACHER'S MEAN, DUDE.
TUK.
TAK TAK TAK TAK TAK TAK TAK TAK TAK TAK TAK TAK TAK

NOT THAT KNOWING EARLY HIGH-SCHOOL MATH IS ANYTHING SPECIAL.
HMM, GOOD. YOU GOT IT RIGHT. YOU MUST BE READING AHEAD.

I'M SO BORED.
IMAMURA!
NO SLEEPING!

WE'RE GOING TO WORK ON VOICE PROJECTION FOR ONE HOUR!
AND YOU BETTER BE LOUD, OR I'LL MAKE IT TWO!
OSU!
OSU!
WUSH
WUSH
WUSH
LOUDER, FIRST-YEARS!
I CAN BARELY HEAR YOU!
LOWER YOUR STANCE!
PANT
PANT
I SAID LOWER! AND STRAIGH-TEN YOUR ARMS!

HEY … EXCUSE … ME …

PANT PANT

PLEASE … CAN I REST… JUST A LITTLE?

M- ME, TOO.

PANT PANT

…

ALL RIGHT.

SIGH

YOU'VE GOT 15 MINUTES. THEN WE'RE TAKING IT FROM THE TOP.

HEEEEY! USAMIII!
HOW'S THE TRAINING GOING?
KITAJIMA-SENSEI.

…

HMM.

THEY ALL LISTEN TO ME.

THEY'RE NOT BAD GUYS …

…BUT SOMEHOW I DON'T GET THE FEELING THEY'RE GIVING THIS THEIR ALL.

I MEAN, THEY'RE JUST SORT OF PASSIVE.

ARE YOU SURE YOU AREN'T BEING TOO HARD ON THEM?
I'M TAKING IT EXTREMELY EASY ON THEM!
I LITERALLY COUGHED UP BLOOD WHEN I WAS NEW TO THE CLUB.
OSU!
OSU!
KOFF
MY SENPAI WOULD'VE LEFT ME HALF-DEAD IF I'D HAVE ASKED FOR A BREAK!
THE KIDS THESE DAYS ARE JUST TOO SOFT!
WHEN I WAS THEIR AGE, WE WERE A LOT STRICTER ABOUT HOW WE SPOKE TO OUR SUPERIORS.
AND THEN THERE'S VOICE PROJECTION! FOR A MEMBER OF THE OUENDAN, THE REAL YELLING DOESN'T START UNTIL YOU'VE LOST YOUR VOICE...
I CAN'T BELIEVE THEY'RE RUNNING OUT OF BREATH OVER A LITTLE BIT OF BASIC ENDURANCE TRAINING!
AND THEY STILL HAVE SO MUCH TO LEARN BEFORE THE INTERCLUB TRAINING!
HEAR ME OUT! EARLIER TODAY...
PLUS...
AND THEN...
HMMMMMM.
WE DON'T HAVE MUCH TIME LEFT UNTIL THE INTERCLUB TRAINING, DO WE?
IT MIGHT BE TOO LATE FOR THEM TO LEARN THE CHOREOGRAPHY FOR OUR BASEBALL CHEERS...
NOT TO MENTION THE TAIKO DRUMMING...
...

OUENDAN
RADIO CLUB
WHY DON'T WE ...
...ASK *THEM* TO COME BACK?
I CAN SEE HOW HARD YOU'RE WORKING, BUT I THINK THE SITUATION CALLS FOR–
THAT WON'T BE NECESSARY.
WE...
...CAN HANDLE THIS OURSELVES!

IS THAT SO?
ALL RIGHT, THEN.
WE'RE STARTING PRACTICE.
EXCUSE ME, BUT IT STILL HASN'T BEEN 15 MINUTES.
WE'RE STARTING.
UH-
OH, OKAY.
YOU MEAN, "OSU!"
KANAAAAN!
FIGHT!
KANAN
MI-NA-MI!
GO! GO! LET'S GO!

THE OUENDAN DOESN'T NEED ME TO SAVE IT ANYMORE.
DUM
DADUM
DADUM
NOW...
DUM
DUM
DUM
...I ALREADY KNOW WHAT THE FUTURE HOLDS.
I GUESS I JUST HAVE TO WAIT FOR IT TO PASS ME BY.
DADUM
DUM
TAP
TATAP
TATAP
DADUM
THREE YEARS OF HIGH SCHOOL.
TATAP
DUM
DADUM
DUM
DADUM
TAP
OVER A THOUSAND DAYS OF BOREDOM.
DUM
DUM
DUM
TAP
TAP
TAP
IMA-MURA-KUN!
THERE YOU ARE.
I'VE BEEN LOOKING FOR YOU!
SO ...
WANNA START HEADING HOME?
SURE.

YOU MUST STUDY A LOT, HUH, IMAMURA-KUN?
YOU SURPRISED ME TODAY, SINCE IT NEVER SEEMED LIKE YOU TOOK CLASS VERY SERIOUSLY.
OH, NAH.
I DON'T REALLY STUDY.

...

LIKE ...
YOU NEVER SEEM VERY MOTIV-ATED.
EH ...

OH ...
HANGING OUT WITH ME MUST BE PRETTY BORING, HUH?

YOU'RE NOT BORING, SHIBATA-SAN.
I JUST ...
...THINK HIGH SCHOOL IS BORING.
GAAAH.
Ugh.
THERE'S NOTHING TO DO.
Y'KNOW ...
MAYBE NOTHING MIND-BLOWINGLY COOL IS EVER GONNA HAPPEN TO ME.

WE ...
... NEED TO TALK.
GRAB

WHAT?

WELL, YOU SEE ...
THERE'S SOME-THING I'VE BEEN WANTING TO TELL YOU.

ARE YOU TRYING TO SCARE ME?

THAT'S RIGHT!

IT'S TIME FOR YOU TO COME CLEAN, REO SHIBATA.

BAM

UHH?

OKAY. SEE YOU GUYS TOMORROW.

BYE.

INTERESTING LITTLE CHAT.

CARE TO FILL ME IN ON THE DETAILS?

...AND THAT'S WHAT'S GOING ON.

SEE?

DON'T YOU GET IT?

IT WAS ALL A SCHEME BY THE CHEERLEADERS' CAPTAIN TO DESTROY THE OUENDAN!

THIS GIRL IS JUST A HONEYPOT!

DON'T MAKE IT SOUND ALL WEIRD!

What were you doing, grabbing his arm?

W-Well, you see...

...

YOU SERIOUSLY THOUGHT THE SMARTEST GIRL IN OUR YEAR WOULD COME ON TO YOU AND YOU COULD MAKE FRIENDS JUST LIKE THAT, HUH?
TURNS OUT TURNING YOUR LIFE AROUND AIN'T THAT EASY.
HAVE I OPENED YOUR EYES?

I JUST ...
I'M SORRY!
I WANTED TO TELL YOU EVENTUALLY ...
BOW!!
BUT, IMAMURA-KUN ...
...I REALLY WOULD LIKE TO HELP YOU OUT, SO-

UH-HUH.
WHATEVER, IT'S FINE.
YOU WERE JUST FOLLOWING ORDERS AND HAD TO EAT LUNCH WITH ME NO MATTER HOW MUCH YOU HATED IT.
NO!
I DIDN'T HATE IT!

AND HERE I THOUGHT I'D HAVE TO LIVE THE SAME BORING THREE YEARS ALL OVER AGAIN.
IMA-MURA?
WAIT...
UHH?
OH GOD... I REALLY UNDER-ESTIMATED THIS WORLD.
WHILE I WASN'T PAYING ATTEN-TION...
HEH HEH
...ALL SORTS OF COOL STUFF WAS GOING ON RIGHT UNDER MY NOSE.

I'VE SPENT THREE YEARS OF MY LIFE BEING TOTALLY IGNORED, SO DON'T YOU DARE UNDER-ESTIMATE ME!
YOU CAN TREAT ME HOWEVER YOU WANT! I'M ALREADY USED TO IT, DUMBASS!

I WILL NOT LET THEM DESTROY THE OUENDAN!
CLAAAANG
NGH...
PAAANG
WHOA...
YOU DORK.
SO...
CAN I GO HOME NOW?

9. THE DIRT ON USAMI

SO, REO-CHAN,
HOW'D YOUR LITTLE AFTER-SCHOOL DATE YESTER-DAY GO?
HAVE YOU AND IMAMURA KISSED YET?
NO, WE HAVEN'T.
WHY NOT? IS HE CELIBATE OR SOME-THING?
HARSH!
MAYBE HE DOESN'T HAVE MUCH OF A SEX DRIVE.
SQUEEEEEEEZE
DID HE SAY ANYTHING ABOUT THE OUENDAN?

IT SOUNDS LIKE HE'S LOST INTEREST.
HE REALIZED CAPTAIN USAMI DIDN'T NEED HIM, AND HE WAS PRETTY UPSET ABOUT IT.
HA HA!
THAT'S FUNNY.
BOYS ARE SUCH SIMPLE CREA-TURES.

USAMI MUST BE SO HAPPY TO HAVE ALL THOSE NEW MEM-BERS.
CAP-TAIN!!
WE ...ANT TO ...HEER WITH ...OU!
I WONDER WHAT THE LOOK ON HER FACE WILL BE IN THREE DAYS WHEN EVERY ONE OF THEM SUBMITS A RESIGNATION FORM ON THE DAY OF OUR INTERCLUB TRAINING.

HE HE HE HE HE
...
ARE YOU ...
...SURE WE'LL BE BETTER OFF WITHOUT THE OUEN-DAN?
EXCUSE ME?
I'M SURE YOU'VE HEARD ...
... ABOUT WHY USAMI IS THEIR LAST MEMBER.

REO-CHAN.
I BELIEVE YOU REALLY ARE ON OUR SIDE.
I'M TRUSTING YOU, OKAY?
WE ONLY HAVE THREE DAYS UNTIL THE CHEERLEADERS' AND OUENDAN'S INTERCLUB TRAINING.
THE BRASS AND WIND BAND AND SOME MEMBERS OF THE BASEBALL CLUB WILL BE PARTICIPATING, AS WELL.
APPARENTLY, THE CAPTAIN OF THE OUENDAN HAS TRADITIONALLY BEEN THE CHEER DIRECTOR, WHO'S RESPONSIBLE FOR ORGANIZING THE DIFFERENT CLUBS TOGETHER.

BUT CAPTAIN USAMI'S BEEN THE ONLY MEMBER OF THE OUENDAN SINCE THE MIDDLE OF LAST YEAR, SO NOW BEING THE CHEER DIRECTOR IS HER ONLY REAL ROLE.
MEAN-WHILE, THE CHEER-LEADING CLUB, WITH SO MANY MORE MEMBERS, HAS BEEN DOING MOST OF THE ACTUAL CHEERING.
KANAN
CAPTAIN ABE ISN'T TOO HAPPY ABOUT THAT,
SO SHE'S ARRANGED FOR THOSE NEW MEM-BERS TO ALL BAIL ON THE DAY OF THE INTERCLUB TRAINING.
Home
About
Student Life
Activities
Ouendan & Cheerleading Club
MAIN PAGE
ACTIVITIES
REPORTS
CLICK
CLICK CLICK
CLICK
CLICK
BASICALLY, SHE'S TRYING TO DESTROY THE OUENDAN'S REPUTATION AND UNDERMINE THEIR AUTHORITY.
PERSONALLY, I THINK WE SHOULD REPORT THIS IMMEDIATELY TO CAPTAIN USAMI, THE OUENDAN'S SPONSOR, AND THE CHEER-LEADING CLUB'S SPONSOR.
LET'S PUT THE ISSUE OUT IN THE OPEN.
WE MIGHT EVEN WANT TO REQUEST THAT THE INTERCLUB TRAINING BE CANCELED.
I *KNEW* A SPY FROM THE CHEER-LEADERS WOULD BE SMART.
YOU'RE AS GOOD AT PLAYING WOMEN AS YOU ARE AT MEN.
HEY!
DON'T CALL ME A SPY!
WHAT ARE YOU GONNA DO, IMA-MURA-KUN?
WE SHOULD TELL SOMEONE ABOUT THIS.
CLICK
CLICK
...

THAT'D BE BORING.

IT WOULD JUST MAKE EVERYONE FEEL LIKE CRAP.

BESIDES, SHIBATA-SAN, YOU'D GET BULLIED BY THE CHEERLEADERS IF THEY FOUND OUT IT WAS YOU WHO SPILLED THE BEANS.

YOU DON'T NEED TO WORRY ABOUT ME.
I'M READY TO DEAL WITH-
WHATEVER.
JUST KEEP ACTING LIKE YOU'RE ON THE CHEERLEADERS' SIDE.

I'LL MAKE IT SEEM LIKE...

...I FIGURED IT OUT ALL ON MY OWN.

TAP TAP

TUNK

TAP TAP

TAP TAP TAP

TAP

IMAMURA-KUN...

YOU'D DO THAT FOR ME?

GAAAAAH, I GOTTA FIND A WAY TO HUMILIATE THAT CHEER CAPTAIN, SOMETHING THAT'LL REALLY MAKE A SPLASH.

DAMN, IMAMURA, YOU REALLY ARE A JERK.

...

LET'S GOOGLE "REVENGE METHODS."

HMM.

HOW ABOUT "PRANKS FOR PAYBACK"?

Ugh.

TUNK

TAP TAP

TAP

TAP TAP

COME TO THINK OF IT, WHY IS CAPTAIN USAMI THE ONLY ONE LEFT IN THE OUENDAN, ANYWAY?
CREEEAK
THERE MUST'VE BEEN SOME OTHER MEMBERS. DO YOU KNOW ANYTHING ABOUT THAT?

WAIT, YOU DON'T KNOW?
KNOW WHAT?

OH, I GET IT. YOU DIDN'T MOVE HERE UNTIL HIGH SCHOOL, RIGHT?
USAMI-SAN IS A BIT OF A LOCAL LEGEND.

DID YOU EVER SEE HER ON TV, FUJIEDA-SAN?
OH YEAH, I GUESS I DID. THEY WERE TALKING ABOUT HER A LOT FOR A WHILE.

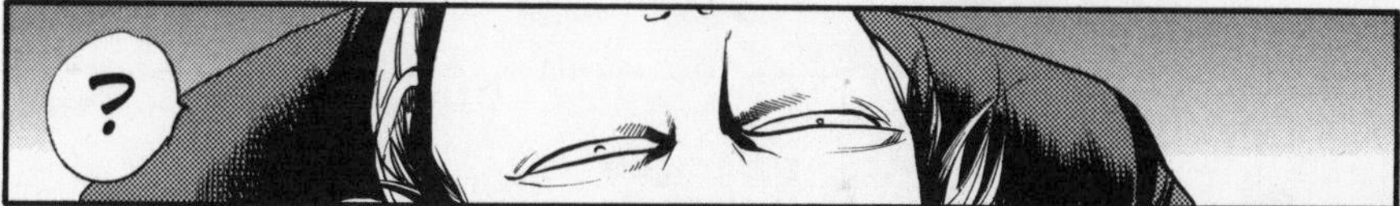
?

TODAY, IN REGIONAL NEWS, WE'LL BE REPORTING ON A TEENAGE GIRL WHO'S A MEMBER OF HER SCHOOL'S OUENDAN!
SPECIAL FEATURE
A DELICATE FLOWER'S OLD FASHIONED CHEERS
TOO CUTE!
A Girl in the Ouendan?!
COULD SHE BE A REAL VERSION OF THE GIRL FROM CHEER CHEER CHEER ?!
FIND OUT AFTER THIS COMMERCIAL BREAK!

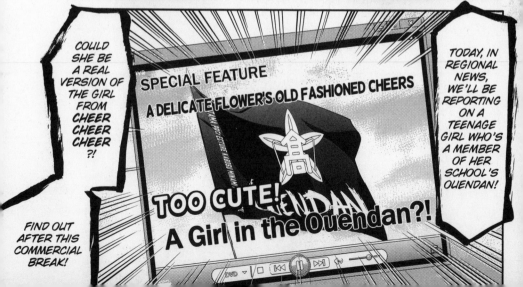

THIS IS IT!
WHAT THE?
WHAT GOT YOU SO INTERESTED...
HEY!
I THINK I MIGHT'VE SEEN THIS.
...IN SEEING THESE RECORDINGS OF THE OUENDAN BEING FEATURED ON THE NEWS?
There's more where that came from!

AT FIRST GLANCE, KABOSU MINAMI HIGH SCHOOL'S YOSHIKO USAMI APPEARS TO BE YOUR AVERAGE TEENAGE GIRL.
QUIET AND SOMETHING OF AN OVERACHIEVER, SHE'S NOT THE KIND OF GIRL WHO TENDS TO STICK OUT.

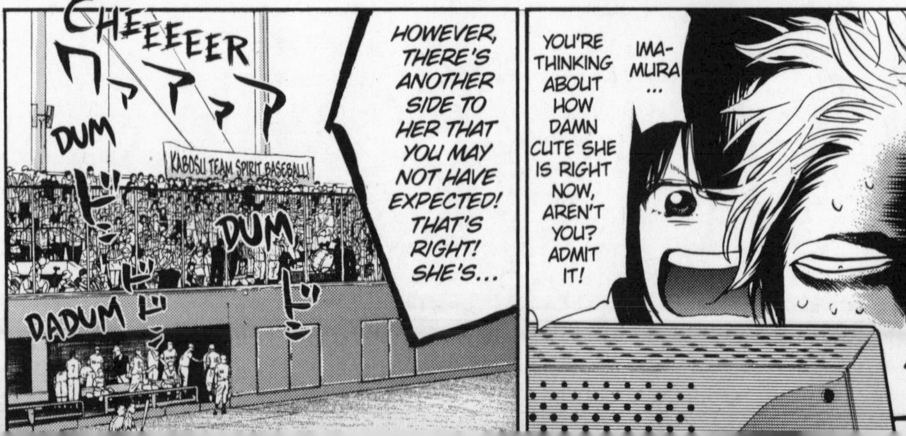
IMAMURA...
YOU'RE THINKING ABOUT HOW DAMN CUTE SHE IS RIGHT NOW, AREN'T YOU? ADMIT IT!
HOWEVER, THERE'S ANOTHER SIDE TO HER THAT YOU MAY NOT HAVE EXPECTED! THAT'S RIGHT! SHE'S...
CHEEEEER
ワァァァア
KABOSU TEAM SPIRIT BASEBALL!
DUM
DUM
DADUM
ドンドンドドン

YOU CAN DO IT!!
NAKAGAWA
...THE FIRST FEMALE MEMBER OF KABOSU MINAMI HIGH'S OUENDAN!
DADUM
DADUM
DADUM
OH, HEY.
SO SHE WASN'T THE ONLY MEMBER.
YOU CAN DO IT!
YOU CAN DO IT!
DADUM
SHE WEARS THE TRADITIONAL BLAZER-AND-SLACKS UNIFORM ALONGSIDE HER MALE CLUBMATES.
AND SHE GETS A LOT OF ATTENTION FOR IT!
NAKAGA
TOO CUTE!
A Girl in the Ouendan?!

WHY DID YOU DECIDE TO JOIN THE OUENDAN WHEN ALL THE OTHER MEMBERS ARE BOYS?
OSU! I WAS MOVED BY THEIR PERFORMANCE AT MY ENTTRANCE CEREMONY! SO I DECIDED TO JOIN!
COULDN'T YOU HAVE JOINED THE CHEER-LEADING CLUB, THOUGH?
OSU!
I WAS MORE INTERESTED IN THE BOYS' OUENDAN!

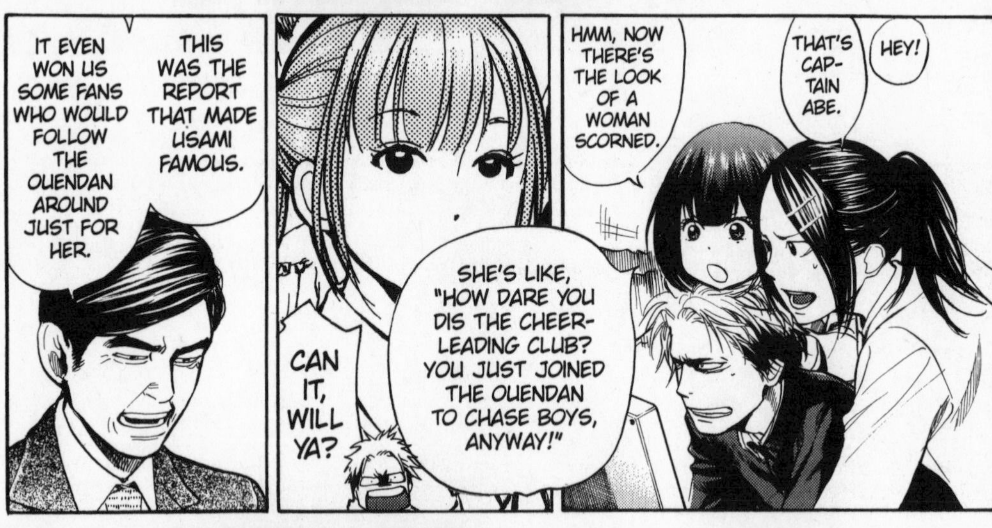
HEY!
THAT'S CAP-TAIN ABE.
HMM, NOW THERE'S THE LOOK OF A WOMAN SCORNED.
SHE'S LIKE, "HOW DARE YOU DIS THE CHEER-LEADING CLUB? YOU JUST JOINED THE OUENDAN TO CHASE BOYS, ANYWAY!"
CAN IT, WILL YA?
THIS WAS THE REPORT THAT MADE USAMI FAMOUS.
IT EVEN WON US SOME FANS WHO WOULD FOLLOW THE OUENDAN AROUND JUST FOR HER.

USAMI WENT ALONG WITH THIS KIND OF THING BECAUSE SHE WANTED TO DO SOMETHING TO HELP THE OUENDAN COME BACK FROM ITS SLOW DECLINE OVER THE YEARS,
BUT THEN PEOPLE STARTED TALKING. THEY'D SAY SHE WAS LETTING THE FAME GO TO HER HEAD OR THAT SHE WAS JUST USING THE OUENDAN.
AND THINGS GOT REALLY BAD FOR HER ONCE SHE BECAME THE TARGET OF AN ONLINE SMEAR CAMPAIGN.
TOO CUTE!
A Girl in the Ouendan?!

WAIT ...
A CERTAIN SOMEBODY MUST HAVE BEEN JEALOUS.
RIGHT?! WHO COULD IT HAVE BEEN?! IT'S JUST HORRIBLE!
STEAM STEAM
HA HA!
THAT SHE HAD BEEN CAUSING PROBLEMS IN THE OUENDAN EVER SINCE SHE STARTED APPEARING ON TV.
ALLEGEDLY, THE OUENDAN PUT ALL THEIR ACTIVITIES ON HIATUS AND JUST ABOUT DISBANDED BECAUSE OF THAT,
SO IN THE END, CAPTAIN USAMI WAS THE ONLY PERSON LEFT IN THE CLUB.
RAGE
Y'KNOW, I HEARD SOME OF THOSE RUMORS MYSELF,
BUT MAYBE THEY WERE JUST A BUNCH OF LIES ...
SERI-OUSLY ?
WHAT WERE THEY ?
PHEW
WHAT THE HELL ?
HOW MUCH OF THAT IS TRUE ?
...
IT'S TRUE THAT USAMI ENDED UP AS THE LAST REMAINING MEMBER OF THE OUENDAN ...
...BUT I ASSURE YOU THAT THOSE RUMORS ARE COMPLETELY BASELESS! DON'T YOU WORRY!
FWOO

IMA-MURA!
USAMI MAY BE A LITTLE STUBBORN AT TIMES...
...BUT THAT DOESN'T CHANGE THE FACT THAT SHE'S IN NEED OF COMPANIONS.
SMACK
SMACK
HELP HER OUT FOR ME.

DADUM
DADUM
GO KANAN!
DADUM
...GO!
DUM
DADUM

THE CAPTAIN WASN'T ALONE IN THE OUENDAN.
THOSE GUYS...
...MUST STILL GO TO SCHOOL HERE.

SO IF THEY JOIN BACK UP, THE OUENDAN DOESN'T HAVE TO FALL APART!

KITA-JIMA-SEN-SEI!
WHO ARE THE FORMER MEMBERS OF THE OUENDAN THAT STILL GO TO SCHOOL HERE?

HUH?

Bye-bye!
See ya!

IT'S NO USE.
WE'RE NOT GONNA FIND KITAJIMA-SENSEI.
ANOTHER TEACHER SAID HE MIGHT HAVE ALREADY GONE HOME.
DAMN IT.
WHAT IS HE TRYING TO HIDE?
IT'S NOT LIKE WE CAN'T FIND OUT WHAT THE FORMER OUENDAN MEMBERS LOOK LIKE BY WATCHING THESE DVDS.
WHAT IF THE OUENDAN'S HIATUS REALLY WAS...
...CAPTAIN USAMI'S FAULT?
YEAH, AND THE FORMER MEMBERS STILL HATE HER FOR IT?
DUM...
DADUM...
...
HEY.
I HEAR THE SOUND OF TAIKO DRUMS.
SOME-ONE MUST BE PRAC-TICING, HUH?
COULD IT BE THE CHEER-LEAD-ERS?
THE OUEN-DAN?
DUM
DADUM
DADUM
DADUM
DUM

DUM
TAP
DA DUM
TA TAP
DUM
TAP
DA DUM
TA TAP
DUM
TAP
MUMBLE
MUMBLE MUMBLE

THE OUEN-DAN'S CAP-TAIN ...
...REALLY CAN'T KEEP A BEAT, CAN SHE?

HEY!
AGH!
GRAB
YOU ...
... PLAYED TAIKO FOR THE OUENDAN, DIDN'T YOU?
BA-DUMP...

OH MY GOD I'M SO SORRY !!
FWOOM
UHHHHH...
HUH?
TO BE CONTINUED IN VOLUME 2!

It's the AFTERWORD!

It's been a while, but I'm back to writing for a shonen magazine. I've wanted to do a comic about an ouendan since I was in high school. Some people will tell me that I've already done that with 3-3-7 Byoshi!!, but all the ouendan did in that comic was die! I didn't get to actually draw the ouendan at all!

I wanted to include modern-day ouendan besides just the one from my old high school in my research, so I went to Fudooka High to gather material. I'd like to thank them for their cooperation! It was mind-boggling to me how clean the school buildings were kept and how nice all the students were.

Now that I'm an adult, there are times when I look back and wish I would have done things differently. I'll be happy if this manga inspires those of you who are in school now—or who will be in the future—to think about how you'll reflect on your current self once you've graduated in a few years!

2011.8. 久保ミツロウ☆

Mitsurou Kubo, August 2011

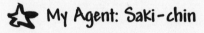

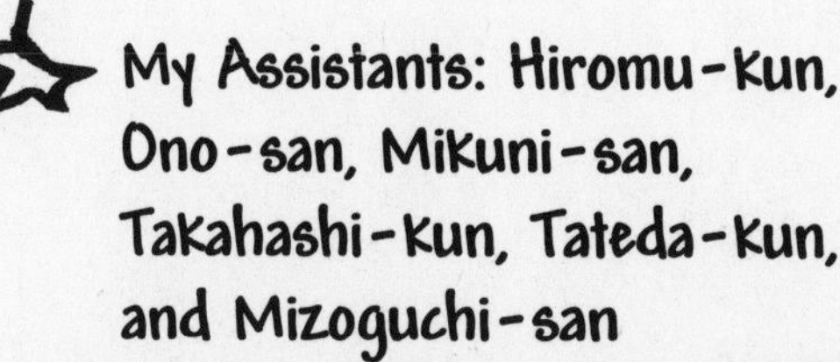

My Assistants: Hiromu-kun,
Ono-san, Mikuni-san,
Takahashi-kun, Tateda-kun,
and Mizoguchi-san

Translation Notes

"The second button of your blazer"
Page 5

At Japanese graduation ceremonies, students will sometimes request that a boy they have feelings for give them the second button of his blazer. The origin of this custom is unclear, but there are a couple of theories as to its meaning. One suggests that it is because this button is close to the boy's heart, while another claims that each button of the blazer represents someone in your life, with the second button representing someone very dear to you.

Senpai and kohai
Page 13

In many Japanese institutions, such as school clubs and corporate offices, the dominant perspective is that you should respect, listen to, and try to imitate the people who have been part of that institution for longer than you have. These people are your *senpai*. Conversely, your *kohai* are junior to you—the people to whom you are a senpai.

Ouendan

Page 17

For those who aren't familiar with the term, an *ouendan* (literally, "cheering group" and pronounced OH-en-dahn) is a kind of club at some Japanese schools that does things like cheering, singing, and playing drums to generate excitement at school events, such as sports games. This term is not interchangeable with something like "cheerleaders," because it carries certain specific implications about the club's style of dress, kinds of performance, and type of management. You might, however, think of it as a sort of pep squad. Typically, ouendan are predominantly male.

Don't call me Hiro-kun

Page 66

In Japanese, the name you call someone says a lot about your relationship with that person. Aki is calling Hiro by his first name, which implies a certain degree of familiarity, and with the suffix *-kun*, which is typically used for people in an equal or lower social position than yourself, depending on the context. In other words, from Hiro's perspective, she's coming on way too strong and being sort of rude.

Osu
Page 75

Those readers who have practiced Japanese martial arts may be familiar with this term, which is usually pronounced OHSS. The origins of the term are unclear, but today, it is sometimes used as an affirmative expression in sports that emphasize discipline. In this context, it is often written with the Chinese characters for "to push," implying a meaning to the effect of "to humbly hone one's skill."

Kanan High
Page 160

This is the abbreviated name of Kinichiro's high school. This abbreviation might make more sense if you take a look at the Chinese characters with which each name is written. The full name of the school is *Kabosu Minami* or **加保須南**, while the abbreviation is **加南**. "Nan" is simply an alternative pronunciation of the character pronounced "minami" in the unabbreviated form. It is often used in compound words. Whereas "Kabosu Minami" is a long and traditional-sounding name, "Kanan" sounds snappy and modern.

Tigers
Page 142

The Japanese title of this chapter makes a pun out of the words "tiger" (*tora*) and "troublemaker" (*toraburu-meikaa*). Incidentally, Reo's name could also be rendered as Leo, Latin for lion.

Cheer Cheer Cheer
Page 185

Cheer Cheer Cheer is a 2008 Japanese movie. It tells the story of a young girl's attempt to revitalize her school's dying *ouendan* in order to get close to a boy she likes.

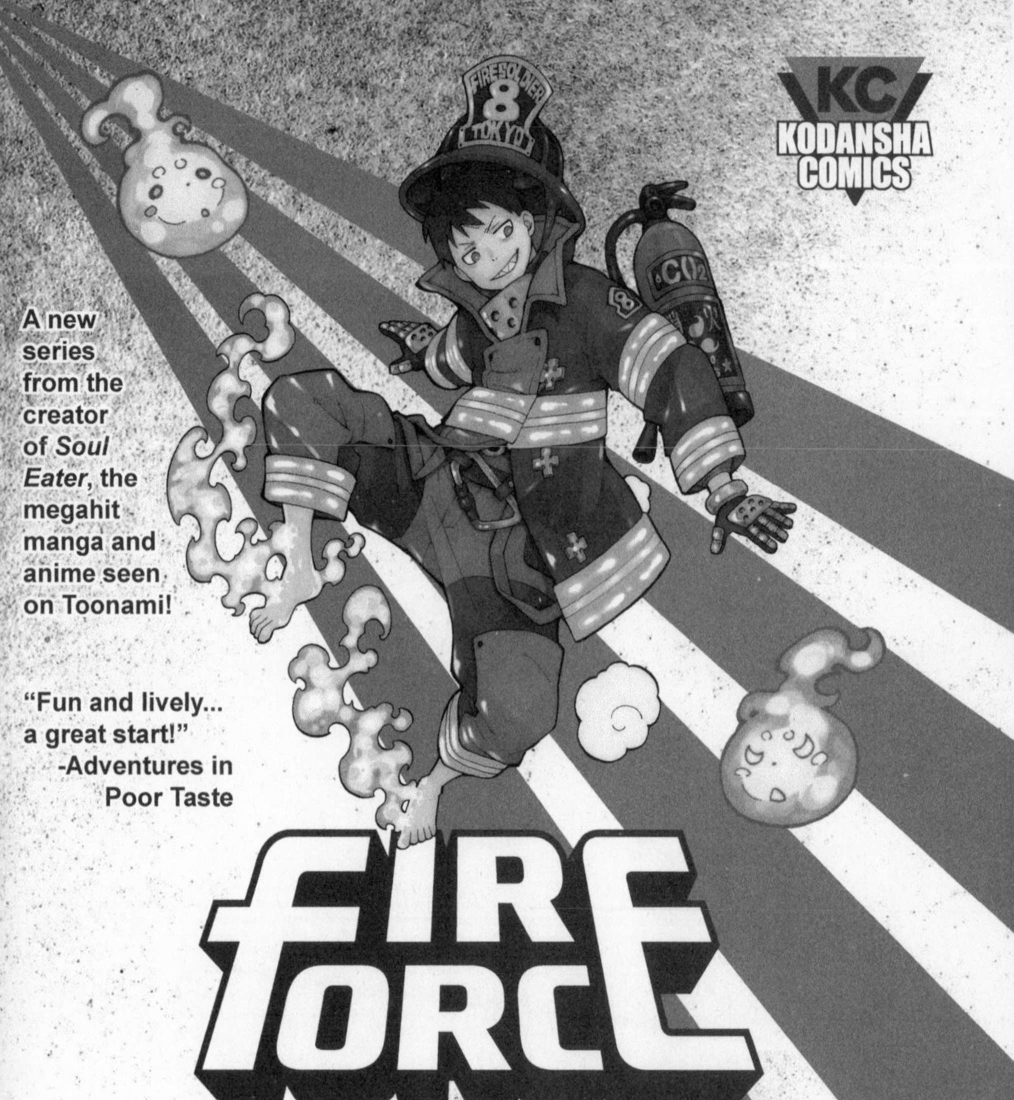

KC
KODANSHA COMICS
FIRE SOLDIER
8
TOKYO
A new series from the creator of *Soul Eater*, the megahit manga and anime seen on Toonami!
"Fun and lively... a great start!"
-Adventures in Poor Taste
FIRE FORCE

By Atsushi Ohkubo

The city of Tokyo is plagued by a deadly phenomenon: spontaneous human combustion! Luckily, a special team is there to quench the inferno: The Fire Force! The fire soldiers at Special Fire Cathedral 8 are about to get a unique addition. Enter Shinra, a boy who possesses the power to run at the speed of a rocket, leaving behind the famous "devil's footprints" (and destroying his shoes in the process). Can Shinra and his colleagues discover the source of this strange epidemic before the city burns to ashes?

HAPPINESS

——ハピネス——

By Shuzo Oshimi

From the creator of *The Flowers of Evil*

Nothing interesting is happening in Makoto Ozaki's first year of high school. His life is a series of quiet humiliations: low-grade bullies, unreliable friends, and the constant frustration of his adolescent lust. But one night, a pale, thin girl knocks him to the ground in an alley and offers him a choice. Now everything is different. Daylight is searingly bright. Food tastes awful. And worse than anything is the terrible, consuming thirst...

Praise for Shuzo Oshimi's *The Flowers of Evil*

"A shockingly readable story that vividly—one might even say queasily—evokes the fear and confusion of discovering one's own sexuality. Recommended." —The Manga Critic

"A page-turning tale of sordid middle school blackmail." —Otaku USA Magazine

"A stunning new horror manga." —Third Eye Comics

The Black Museum
The Ghost and the Lady

By Kazuhiro Fujita

Deep in Scotland Yard in London sits an evidence room dedicated to the greatest mysteries of British history. In this "Black Museum" sits a misshapen hunk of lead–two bullets fused together–the key to a wartime encounter between Florence Nightingale, the mother of modern nursing, and a supernatural Man in Grey. This story is unknown to most scholars of history, but a special guest of the museum will tell the tale of The Ghost and the Lady...

Praise for Kazuhiro Fujita's *Ushio and Tora*

"A charming revival that combines a classic look with modern depth and pacing... **Essential viewing both for curmudgeons and new fans alike.**" — Anime News Network

"**GREAT!** The first episode of Ushio and Tora captures the essence of '90s anime." — IGN

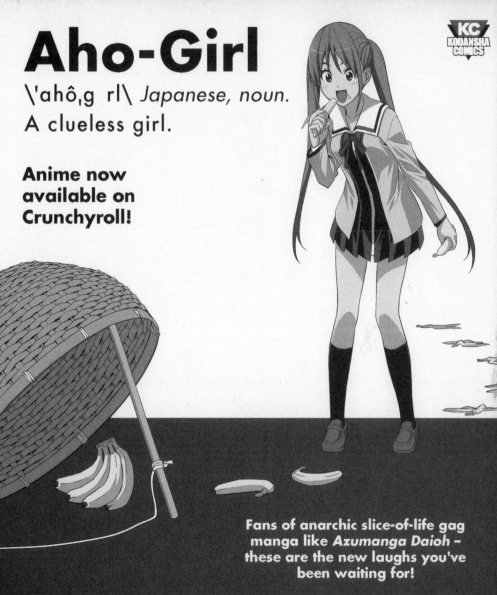

"I'm pleasantly surprised to find modern shojo using cross-dressing as a dramatic device to deliver social commentary... Recommended."

-Otaku USA Magazine

the prince in his dark days

By Hico Yamanaka

A drunkard for a father, a household of poverty... For 17-year-old Atsuko, misfortune is all she knows and believes in. Until one day, a chance encounter with Itaru–the wealthy heir of a huge corporation–changes everything. The two look identical, uncannily so. When Itaru curiously goes missing, Atsuko is roped into being his stand-in. There, in his shoes, Atsuko must parade like a prince in a palace. She encounters many new experiences, but at what cost…?

KC KODANSHA COMICS

A beautifully-drawn new action manga from Haruko Ichikawa, winner of the Osamu Tezuka Cultural Prize!

LAND OF THE LUSTROUS

In a world inhabited by crystalline life-forms called The Lustrous, every gem must fight for their life against the threat of Lunarians who would turn them into decorations. Phosphophyllite, the most fragile and brittle of gems, longs to join the battle, so when Phos is instead assigned to complete a natural history of their world, it sounds like a dull and pointless task. But this new job brings Phos into contact with Cinnabar, a gem forced to live in isolation. Can Phos's seemingly mundane assignment lead both Phos and Cinnabar to the fulfillment they desire?

A Kodansha Comics Trade Paperback Original.

Published in the United States by Kodansha Comics, an imprint of Kodansha USA Publishing, LLC, New York.

Publication rights for this English edition arranged through Kodansha Ltd., Tokyo.

First published in Japan in 2011 by Kodansha Ltd., Tokyo, as *Agein!!* volume 1.

ISBN 978-1-63236-645-0

Printed in the United States of America.

www.kodanshacomics.com

9 8 7 6 5 4 3 2 1

Translator: Rose Padgett
Lettering: E. K. Weaver
Lettering Assistance: James Dashiell
Editing: Paul Starr and Jesika Brooks
Editorial Assistance: Tiff Ferentini
Kodansha Comics edition cover design by Phil Balsman

EVEN NOW, THREE YEARS LATER, I STILL THINK ABOUT HER SOME-TIMES.
WHAT WOULD THINGS BE LIKE IF I HAD ACCEPTED HER OFFER?
THEN AGAIN... DOES IT REALLY MATTER ANYMORE?
NO, IT'S TOO LATE.
BESIDES...

...MY AGONIZINGLY LONG HIGH-SCHOOL CAREER ENDS TODAY.
1. CONGRATULATIONS, GRADUATE

Mitsurou Kubo
Again!!
アゲイン!!
No.
1

contents